Open-Hearted Horizon

An Albuquerque Poetry Anthology

open-hearted horizon

EDITED BY *Valerie Martínez*

AND *Shelle VanEtten de Sánchez*

University of New Mexico Press

Albuquerque

City of Albuquerque Department of Arts & Culture

ISBN 978-0-8263-6621-4 (paper
ISBN 978-0-8263-6622-1 (ePub)

Library of Congress Control Number: 2023951870

Founded in 1889, the University of New Mexico sits on the traditional homelands
of the Pueblo of Sandia. The original peoples of New Mexico—Pueblo, Navajo, and
Apache—since time immemorial have deep connections to the land and have made
significant contributions to the broader community statewide. We honor the land
itself and those who remain stewards of this land throughout the generations and
also acknowledge our committed relationship to Indigenous peoples. We gratefully
recognize our history.

Cover and frontispiece photograph by Robert Carrol Ellis (1923 [Jacksboro, TX]–1979
    [Albuquerque, NM]), Untitled, 1975. Lithograph on paper (22/35), 22 ×
    29 ¾ in. Albuquerque Museum, gift of Frank McCulloch, Patricia, and family.
    PC2021.75.23.
Designed by Isaac Morris
Composed in Arial Rounded, Cronos, and Scala

Contents

Part Four. STRANGE TRANSFORMATIONS

Part Eight. OUR NAMES ARE WATER, OUR NAMES ARE MUD:
A Collaborative Poem—Our Collective Voice—with Lines from
All the Poems in This Collection 163

Preface

Poetry as a Pathway to Liberation

Albuquerque, since its founding, has been a central corridor for writers of all stripes. Fiction writers, mystery megastars, journalists extraordinaire, and poets have traveled our streets and made their home here. Literary history's giants—from Tony Hillerman and our beloved Rudolfo Anaya to the first Native Poet Laureate, Joy Harjo, and the famous war correspondent, Ernie Pyle—have told the stories of Albuquerque and its people. This is our history, and it is also our present as many luminary writers and poets call Albuquerque home today.

Poetry is an enduring component of our public sphere and community forums here in Albuquerque and beyond. Indeed, poetry is a pathway to liberation. One of Albuquerque's greatest poets, Rudolfo Anaya, said, "All literature, especially poetry and fiction, challenges the status quo. That is what literature should do: liberate."[1] Poetry performs a vital social function by telling our stories. It peeks into our city and our world's darkest corners, weathering social storms and political currents, and speaks truth to power. It also uncovers how we are connected and celebrates beauty in all its forms.

Albuquerque's poets have been and continue to be some of the city's hardest-working advocates for liberation. Many of our poets also work in other important sectors of our city—in education, leadership, medicine, law, and more. As the mayor, I have actively recruited and hired poets and other artists into positions of leadership because they bring a creative lens to the problems we face and present us with new opportunities and solutions. Our team has tried to demonstrate that the work of artists is professional work and should be financially compensated just as with any profession. This has led to increased paid opportunities for creatives to work with and within city government through CityMakers, the Artists at Work partnership, and new initiatives developed through Albuquerque's Urban Enhancement Trust Fund. The work our poets do in service to the community has always endured, and since 2012 it has had an official capacity through our City of Albuquerque Poet Laureate program. Our poet laureates have been some of our city's most vocal activists, a point we do not shrink away from, because we know the immense value of free expression and diverse voices. Celebrating creative and free expression, the Albuquerque Poet Laureate program to date has given our city's residents the opportunity to work with six of the finest New Mexico poets on a multitude of free programs and poetry events all over the city.

Albuquerque's poetry scene has been strong since the late 1950s, beginning with vibrant and regular gatherings and readings in independent bookstores and coffeehouses downtown and near the University of New Mexico and continuing across decades. This long tradition includes a wide range of series, such as Adobe Walls Open Mic, Speak Poet: Voz, Palabra y Sonido, Sunday Chatter, Duende Poetry Series, Jules' Poetry Playhouse, East of Edith, Fixed and Free, Wordspace, Poetry and Beer, Wordstream, 516 Words, and more. ABQ Slams (1994–present) has hosted performance poetry events and sponsored local poets to travel and perform nationally and internationally while producing the 2005 National Poetry Slam Champions and the 2013 and 2016 National Poetry Slam Group Piece Champions. As the mayor of Albuquerque, people in other cities (like Detroit) have asked me about (and heaped praise upon) Albuquerque's winning Poetry Slam Teams and individual champions. Poetry is one of many things that Albuquerque does well, and it represents one of our most celebrated forms of storytelling.

Our city's investment in poetry and literature through the Albuquerque Poet Laureate program and through book publishing partnerships like this one with the University of New Mexico Press further validates and preserves the words of our poets as a pathway to freedom. Our poetry projects provide snapshots of our city at every turn, documenting for posterity a history that only poets can capture so precisely.

In the day of increased book banning and as fires of censorship burn on, books matter more than ever, and poets continue to act as a force for liberation. In his essay, "Take the Tortillas Out of Your Poetry," Anaya asks where censorship begins and what are its methods of commission and omission. Indeed, at that time, Chicano authors and writers like Anaya were being asked by the publishing industry to "leave out the tortillas." As Anaya explains, to take out the tortillas means that "the language, history, cultural values, and themes of our literature, the very culture we're portraying, will die."[2]

This anthology adds to New Mexico's poetic history by bringing an extensive (but never complete) volume of local work by living poets into a contemporary, representative collection that preserves our rich Albuquerque culture. Our history is proclaimed and punctuated by the words of our poets. May the poetry included here be a pathway to peace, prosperity, and ponderance as we move forward as a city together, with the powerful words of our poets in our ears and in our hearts.

Tim Keller, Mayor of Albuquerque
December 2022

Notes

1.   Rudolfo Anaya, "Take the Tortillas Out of Your Poetry," in *The Essays* (Norman: University of Oklahoma Press, 2015).

2.   Anaya, "Take the Tortillas."

Introduction

A Conversation between the Editors

Open-Hearted Horizon invites you into a poetic conversation. Included here are many poems by many poets, and all are inspired—directly, associatively, or obliquely—by Albuquerque, New Mexico, as a place and as a community. Anthologies celebrate a multitude of voices. Because this one is place-based, we hope you will feel drawn into a circle that deepens your sense of place and people, of contexts and cultures, whether you know Albuquerque or not. In this spirit, we invite you into the conversation that gave birth to this collection and inspired us to offer these Albuquerque poems to you.

Valerie Martínez: Whenever I see a new poetry anthology I think, *Why this anthology, and why now?*

Shelle Sánchez: Good questions. And this one—Albuquerque poets, poems about Albuquerque—what started us down this road?

V: Well, we started thinking about a long, bright thread, a lineage of Albuquerque poetry anthologies—*Voices from the Rio Grande* (1976), *The Indian Rio Grande* (1977), *A Bigger Boat: The Unlikely Success of the Albuquerque Poetry Slam Scene* (2008), *¿de Veras? Young Voices from the National Hispanic Cultural Center* (2009), *Poetry from the Other Side* (2013), *Rolling Sixes Sestinas* (2016), and *That Poet is Dope* (2020).

S: And we shouldn't forget the many Albuquerque poets who are featured in anthologies of New Mexico poetry—*New Mexico Poetry Renaissance* (1994), the *Adobe Walls* series (2010), and the *New Mexico Poetry Anthology* (2022).

V: There's the newest one, the anthology edited by Albuquerque's fifth Poet Laureate, Mary Oishi, featuring poets and poems that were part of her wonderful community project, "Poets in the Libraries."

S: It sounds like our job has been done for us. Oops. [*Laughter.*] But didn't we feel that a more comprehensive anthology was overdue? Especially for a city that has been such a busy hub for poetry for such a long time.

V: What I love about Albuquerque, what is special about it, I think, is that it's a community that embraces poets and poetries of all kinds—from formal and modern to postmodern, experimental, performance, spoken word, and slam. All manage to coexist and thrive at the same time.

S: It's also a place where poets—across styles and modes and subject matters—lean toward mutual support and collaboration. On any given weekend night, in any one of the many Albuquerque coffeehouses and bars that feature poetry, you will find so-called literary or page poets sitting alongside performance, spoken word, and slam poets.

V: And they often collaborate—composing collective works for readings and performances that promote the idea that poetry is as much a community act as a solitary endeavor. We feature some of these collaborations in this anthology.

S: Yes, lots of introverts willing to create together while still producing their own, individual work. It's the reason why we decided to write this introduction together.

V: It's special. It always has been. It seemed appropriate to honor that by collaborating here.

S: There's also the sheer number of poetry events happening on a daily basis. It's been happening for years. Do you remember that essay in the *Alibi* by Larry Goodell?

V: More than ten years ago. Wasn't it called "Poetry Cake"? I love that title.

S: I happen to have the article right here, at my fingertips. [*Laughter.*] He wrote, "In coffeehouses like the Purple Turk across from Johnson Gym, Louis Greenfield's Bookstore & Coffeehouse downtown, The Grave near Old Town, poetry readings started to pop up here in Albuquerque following the San Francisco Renaissance in the late '50s. The University [of New Mexico] reading performances such as Allen Ginsberg in the Anthropology Hall packed to the ceiling energized young poets. Robert Creeley teaching at UNM was a magnet for poets as was his home in Placitas visited constantly by major poets crossing the country. Bookstores—the Yale Street Grasshopper run by Phil Mayne which turned into the Living Batch Bookstore, Salt of the Earth & Full Circle Bookstores—featured almost endless readings & gatherings."

V: And, until the pandemic, this vibrancy pretty much continued. Think of all the more recent reading series: Adobe Walls Open Mic, Speak Poet: Voz, Palabra y Sonido, Sunday Chatter, Duende Poetry Series, Jules'

Poetry Playhouse, East of Edith, Fixed and Free, Wordspace, Poetry and Beer, Wordstream, 516 Words.

S: All the slam poetry, too! Since 1994 ABQ Slams has hosted performance poetry events and sponsored local poets to travel and perform nationally and internationally. Think of all the championships: Burque poets were the 2005 National Poetry Slam Champions and the 2013 and 2016 National Poetry Slam Group Piece Champions.

V: Then there are the EKCO collaborations—small groups of women poets co-creating collaborative and performance poems since 2009.

S: And, for the last thirteen years, the Albuquerque Poet Laureate Program has selected six Albuquerque Poets Laureate who have reached thousands of city residents with poetry and community-outreach projects.

S: So, I guess we're saying that there could never be too many Albuquerque poetry anthologies?

V: We need many to reflect all the poets and poems and readings and collaborations that make up the poetic "signature" of Albuquerque.

S: What pops out, for you, about this one?

V: Well, we've tried to feature a wide range of work and styles and voices. By putting out an open call, we wanted as many different kinds of poets and poems as possible.

S: For example, take "In Bernalillo, A Blessing" by Jules Nyquist appearing beside "Miso" by Michelle Otero.

V: Such different poems, as if we're saying poetry has room for this much difference, this much variety, this much range. It's exciting.

S: And we avoided sections that had traditional themes in favor of groups of poems that seemed to resonate less obviously and more poetically.

V: What I love best about poetry—indirection. Not linear, not obvious, not simplistic.

S: One of my favorite groupings is "In the Year of Our Peril" (Sylvia Ramos Cruz), "Pandemic Fatigue" (Jenna L. Norton), and "prophesy on an Albuquerque day" (Mary Oishi) in the section "Paths Cut Through the Dry Earth." Poems that evoke life during the COVID-19 pandemic.

V: The section "Never Giving Up Our Roots" with its different takes on the idea of "roots"—Levi Romero's "Azucarero," Greg Candela's "Monarch," Megan Baldrige's "Unendangered Weeds," and Carolyn Fresquez's "I Walk Today, Alone."

S: Yes, and the two sections that evoke two different Albuquerques: "Strange Transformations" and "Sky Kingdom"—vending machines, supermarket carts, and Route 66, and monsoons, the bosque, and the Sandia Mountains. We included several collaborative poems—three by EKCO, creating spoken word performances since 2009, and one in the last section that includes a line from every poem in the anthology.

V: I love that last poem—the anthology's collective poetic voice.

S: I don't think this has been done!

V: So here are our answers: Why an Albuquerque anthology? Because this busy, beautiful place of poetry needs more anthologies to showcase its diversity, its vibrance, its aliveness. And we want to invite residents, visitors, and those who've never been to Albuquerque into this circle.

S: Why now? It's 2024—let's showcase the contemporary Albuquerque poetic community, which gets better every year.

V: It's big, too, and open-hearted.

S: Yes, an open-hearted horizon.

V: I hope readers enjoy this book as much as we do. Here's a toast to the poets and poetry of today's Albuquerque, with our thanks to a long lineage into the past.

S: Bravo!

Part One

The Names We Give These Spaces

Prayer to the Heat

Tanesia R. Hale-Jones

This is a river song
A song of witness: lament and magic
A slow dance along the edges
Brushing against coyote willow
Beetles on pinky fingers

And the heat is in your hair
Rubbing the soft of nostrils
Filling up the throat
Materializing like glitter on concrete
Sliding under the door jamb
A pulse in your stomach to remind you of its humid presence

Children walk on water here
Out across the glass of late afternoon
Sirens gather
Wash your hair, layer mud upon mud and grow tall
This is a kind of communion
Places made for no one in particular
Yet we claim them
(As though that changes something about time)
Circles have been dangerous since time immemorial

In dreams a girl is carried away down river
In reality a girl is carried away down river
Her mother dives after her. Her mother is a root embedded
Wrapping her girl child in gnarled river-stained arms
A river song cooing us to peace
We are not stones, you and I, but dazzling tiny fish
The sand caressing our sticky bodies
What do you call dreams that believe themselves into being
That struggle for foothold among the miraculous everyday
I am standing on the shore watching and calling you back
The others are mirage

I would like to learn to be more riverine
More walkways that come and go
More invitation and various currents
More blanched rocks like teeth and fossil
More islands of refuge
More heat on the floor
More smoky plumes of brown
More retreat and never you mind
Could I be silt and ash
Sage and dust
Both distant and turbulent
Barely there and yet miles long spilling toward a salty other
To play at the boundaries

How do you learn to let go
How do you learn to survive drought
The seasons that char you
Scar and dismantle
What are the locations of pink flowers called
Islands of hope
Reminders that we pay attention differently at dusk
Where did I learn about time
What do we call the spaces that hold drifts of cottonwood seeds sprung
open like bursts of light
What is the name you will give these spaces in your own being
Where are the partitions between worldly and ethereal in which possibility
is held

I would like to be mirage and spectacle
Dry parched spaces, peeling
Mud flats and cool dampness for tiny toads
And doesn't possibility demand friction
I slow and evaporate and allow this or that to die away, this or that to grow
out of the blankness
I break against myself, isn't this what we say
The heat breaks.
I break, and then something else happens

Las Madrecitas de Barelas

María L. Leyba

They had no magic powers
no healing herbs to calm
our locura their faces
would never grace
barrio stucco walls
que vergüenza they would
have said never imagining
they were special
just simple madrecitas
endlessly working from
sunrise to sunset
who loved us dearly
our chantes filled with
an abundance of love/happiness.

Now in our tercera edad
we meet for lunch in coffee
houses or someone's kitchen
blessing our saintly mamas
praying a novena/blessing
their sweet memories.

Some Madrecitas were
Girl Scout leaders others
taught us to cook/sew/embroider.
Polly's mom always cooked
delectable food on a wood stove
while tenderly holding babies
of vecinas. Rosie's mom
the master gardener
had a thrift store in her
dining room. Stella's mom
welcomed us with a huge smile/
homemade bread.

Our mama novena goes on
for hours Madrecitas
who gave us so much
cariño/amor where
our tears stain the tablecloth.

Nothing Was What it Pretended

Margaret Randall

Words I'd never heard took up residence
in my mouth.
Montaño, even if city signage
refused to put the tilda over the n,

names like *De Vargas, Cabeza de Vaca*
or *Juan Tabó*, shepherds and assassins
enshrined on street corners
unquestioned and mispronounced.

Indian words like *Acoma, Navajo*—now *Diné*—
or place names like *Canyon de Chelly*
the conquerors left us with
when they couldn't speak what they couldn't hear.

Names imposed: *Oñate, Coronado, Santa Fe.*
Another's holy faith bringing death
and leaving division, delighting
those who arrive on private planes.

Common words like *tijeras* and *frijoles*,
scissors and beans
began to quiver on my tongue,
stood easily in later years.

I too came from somewhere else,
a childhood far away,
with other sounds in my ears,
other familiars in my mouth.

The new words tested teeth, stretched lips
and exercised my landscape
until language caught meaning in its net
and I knew nothing was what it pretended.

When We Speak Gujarati

Anushah Jiwani

There are pauses. There is softness.
It's not the Gujarati you see in desi films,
Where an uncle with a thick mustache demands chai
as he stuffs himself with dhokla.
There is eye contact. Maybe this is just our Gujarati.
There are intimate relations for women: say
Mummy, bhen, There are stories intertwined
in the sentences, the questions. It's as if the Urdu words
have gentle wrappings, shawls around them.
In our family, Gujarati is spoken on my mom's side. I hear
respect, a quietness. When I try to learn it, it feels broken,
disconnected. For them, it comes out in waves.
In English, Mom says New Mexico reminds her
of home. She looks at the valleys and mountains expanded
and breaths in a different air. At night the hot billowing winds
sound like our ginans, with the voices of hundreds in submission
sung in spirals. The stories of devotion, these Persian words of Pirs,
who traveled from Iran to India, are fused
with Gujarati, Hindi, and Panjabi. We carry this history in our mouths.

Matriz

Michelle Otero

No one is calling. I've ripped the land-
line from the wall, abandoned a home—

no forward address. If children,
they won't know where to live.

We were the place of strays. Pit bull
at the gate. Orange kitten in the garden, scratching soil.

She made litter of manzanilla.
Chicken wandered into our half-acre.

We named her Hungry. Called her
Lady when she turned from kitchen scraps.

Fall she sat on a clutch of eggs. I doused her in cold water
to spare her illusions of birth.

One night raccoon or skunk—
I couldn't save her.

Perhaps I am mother, after all.

The Anthropologist

Anushah Jiwani

Late at night, at 25, I feel like an anthropologist looking
for evidence. The white publisher in Taos wants me to write
through my pain. Find the knowledge before the deadline.
Dad explains Dada and Dadi's migration
stories, and I check Wikipedia to confirm the dates, contexts.
I want to print maps of nations, draw the travels by years. One place
with many names: India, Pakistan, Bangladesh, Kashmir. I want to get it linear,
to make it all make sense. Find the person who cut our land and let it bleed.
I try to track where I come from, borders to match my veins.

What I know
is not much
I'll start with this memory:

My father stands in all black
Nike sweats and a liquor shirt, shining
In the New Mexico sun.   It's early fall
The chlorine dries as our skin whitens   dries.
I sit, legs hanging off the hatchback of the Pathfinder
                        like legs once swinging up to the pink
                        sunset, then back to his soft, solid touch in
                        the park.
He quotes Rumi at least once during our talks.
Sometimes Shams makes his way in, or Gibran.
He tells me
Everything is happening for me. I created my world forty years ago, in my
mind. I believed it,
I became it.
How to change others? Surrender.
            I'm carrying a load of questions: what can
            community accountability look
            like

（so what happened to me does not happen again）

He was fifteen when his brother overdosed, sixteen when he punched
a hole in the living room wall, seventeen when his father died.
                              Do you feel you're doing enough
for the community?
He says I am nobody.

I can't imagine his body at boyhood.
I know the basics—
              crooked teeth from the sharp cricket ball,
              scars on his hand from the textile
factory.   Mustache, thin,   body, thin—too thin;   nation, thin.

I can sense his energy—it reaches me before he does.
Somehow the New Mexico sun begins to heal us.
We part with soft hugs and thank you's. I ask the universe to keep him alive.
                              I can't remember everything he's given me.

Do you feel your heart open?
                        What new future can you imagine?

A Race We Run

Billy Babb

Overhead, *Bien Mur*, Big Mountain
entices with the evening's watermelon promise
Feldspar pink at sunset but verdant now at sunup
Las Sandias jut abruptly above a watery bosque rift

Tendrils of trail twist and wind a twine of dirt
umber and ocher and rose
Underfoot, earth crystals crunch while
lungs labor and
feet   measure   out
a single-track cadence

The mountain stares west at volcanic cousins
indifferent to human struggles below
La luz of the day burns lactic acid and sunlight
as the urgent trail and elevation climb from desert to forest

Slogging, racing, alternately shivering and sweating
ecosystems and altitude strip the oxygen from the air
Jelly legs scramble up and over scree, talus, and rockslide boulders
that taunt ligaments with the prospects of rolling, twisting, tearing

Nineteen switchbacks deposit the determined
still, impossibly
below an aspen encrusted crest
Closer now, cowbells beckon a runner
up a staircase, past well-wishers who taunt "almost there"

A quarter-mile higher, the trail tops out
relenting
with welcoming sunlight
warming

The runner trudges to a stop, atop
permagrin across his face
basking in the satisfaction of high-alpine deliverance

Empty Sky in October

Cal Reardon

I miss the sky-mosaic,
geometric tiles on a backdrop of
deep, wild, open blue;
ever-shifting, turning, lifting
hypnotism; each dust-mote drifter
an atrium of bird-wing vibrancy,
integral to the picture
of the desert kaleidoscope.
Each tile is a flag,
a proclamation of innovation,
a saddle to ride the wind.
Each dragon-breath roar
a cry of defiance against gravity
and borders, a joyful leap
across the cerulean reaches,
a song of loosed latches and
expert gloves over careful patches,
and our diligent hands gently catch
their bodies of wicker and leather
when they fall silent.

Eclipse

Susan Mitchell

Planes are flying
Overhead
Curling
Outworn
Worn out
Dry desert corporation
Pod pot mid-section
Waiting for the wings to break
Off this bouncing belly plane.
And the Sun like
A snot-nosed bratty kid
Ready to grab a weighty pregnant rat
By the tail
And turn it up
And wrong side round
Threatening
All the babies would fall to the ground
And be ruined on the rocks
In tiny twisted broken shapes
With eyelids, limbs and jaws to break.

The white-hot summer Moon is melting.
The face of a tired man
With hair that advertises
"Trim it over the Years, Ma'am,
To the collar please."
A sky passenger
Pulled and pinned to his seat
With a glossy Fortune magazine.
Thus his pride will be spoiled by Freud
Like a taciturn juvenile
Budding sociopath that
Antagonized his father
And his mother loved it

Neurotic henceforth more erotic
Long suffering mother-figure.

New Mexico suffered radiation sickness,
A small boy with all of those responsibilities
Front row seat to the end of the war.
Now we're burning more pockets than ever
Running wells and rivers into chalky dust.
Grins masking sadness on every corner
Gentleman at the Venus Fair.
The desert truly believed heat
Would burn anything
Not everything down everywhere.

Some of us have things
Inside that can freeze the sun.
Holes wear into anything real fast.
Knocking down playing cards with a
Cheap shot.

This century organizes
And retains assaults
Against everything
Vital to invention:
Rubber, safety-pins, screws,
Tubes, bellows, air-brakes, balloons
Lathe, lens, matches, paper and looms
And because of that
The Desert believes its
Fever has a certain ring
Of protest to it.
To dig holes in the
Ground
And navigate
Nature's occasional egg.

Can't Stop

Valerie Martínez

This too is Fire—mirror
    on the mountain. Wet slip
of rock. Sunset. A hiker
    descends the Sandias,
red-orange reflective strips
    aflutter.

Too. Sky. Tiny puddle
    between trunk
and rock. Blue as blue,
    a bridge. Who
stepped here? Fox. Deer
    before a drizzle.
Who brought the sky
    down?

Drought makes an island.
    Pre-teens leap
from riverbank to sand-
    bar. Drop. Measure sky.
Río rounds them, then
    a noisy river patrol.
Sand-angels twinge, cupping
    their ears. Heels dug
way way way in.

Peel up the city-skin
    inch-by-inch. Cursive
of tunnels. Ants, worms,
    moles, millipedes..
Land book. Earth language.
    You, Sun. Ever-reader.

No one said flatness
  is flat, Mesa. You,
are undulance, brimming.
  Heat and dust
radiating their ochre
  somnambulance.

Smoke. No no. Fire
  in the Bosque.
If we were water-bodies.
  If we lay these bodies
down. Tree, brush,
  singed porcupine.
Hissing flames, a slick
  extinguishing.

Come down. Lie down.
  Mirror, cup, balm.
I have loved you, City.
  Dogged. Can't stop.

ABQ Manifesto

Hakim Bellamy

We be
a bucket of Rio,
two handfuls of mesa,
an open box full of God
between the Sandias
and the volcanoes
our name is mud.

We be
close enough to heaven
and clear enough of sky
for the creator
to mouth-to-mouth us alive.

We make dirty
the new "immaculate,"
make car washes obsolete.

We be
urban farmlands
for rural app developers,
be the best brewed beans
and microbrew
in a six-mesa radius . . .

in a hundred mañana radius.

We be coffee shop crushes
and conversations.

We be the creme de la creatives.
We powder with pollen

and monsoon foundation for makeup,
on the rare occasion we "make up,"
only when the winter white tablecloths the mesa.

We be aquifers
of brown gold.
We be the same colored souls.

We be an open-heart horizon.
transplants, land grants,
and colonial survivors.

We be
people of the earth
and out of the world

at the same time.
We inherit this pride.
the "keep it real" estate of intellectual property.

We B-Q-U-E-R-Q-U-E, aye!

We be
sunsets so beautiful
they paint themselves
on the edge of the earth.

We be
where dreams come to live
and retire.

We be
artists making careers
out of thin air.

We be
made-up words like
"Sunport."

Because stars gotta land somewhere?
Because the center of the universe
has gotta be somewhere?
Because even "the sun"
has a vacation home in New Mexico.
Because we be made upwards
not down words
like mountaintop, we be

adobe inside and out.
We might look like
armored vegetarians, but on the inside
we be the coolest *gatas* you'll ever meet.

We be
entrepreneurs and doers.
somewhere between bright ideas and
"done and done."

We be
chile by blood and balloon for lungs.

We be
no "i" in team, but two in familia.

We be full moons and photosynthesis,
not a cloud to be found.

We be radiant.
worshiping the skis
with hand signs that 5-oh-5
to remind our unidentified flying cousins
that we out here,
fighting for our light.

We be loco.
We local.
We be lobos
singing to the night.

We are your favorite city's
favorite city.

The heart of the Southwest
leaning just a li'l to the left
in New Mexico's chest.

Part Two

Never Giving Up Our Roots

Azucarero

Levi Romero

I

¿Qué hay de nuevo pa la Vela?
I ask the young man standing behind
The convenience store cash register,
With a plexiglass shield between us.
It's the same ol' same ol', he tells me,
Just a different generation.

At a historical marker five miles up the road,
I stop to take a picture of the Río Grande.
The mighty Río Bravo del Norte
Still follows the carved path
Laid out by several million years
Of wind and rain and tectonic eruptions.

Tucked into a hollow at the base of the marker
Is a Virgen de Guadalupe votive candle vase
Stuffed with a thin stemmed solar light
And a bundle of red silk tulips.
A month ago someone from our village
Died in a head-on automobile accident here.
Que en paz descanse nuestro primo-paisano.

One side of the historical marker serves as
A Points of Interest map of the Pueblo and Indio-Hispano villages,
Churches, and ancient ruins along the Camino Real.
It is the ancient road also known as El Camino de Agua
Because it was the water route the nuevos pobladores
Followed as they made their way up from Zacatecas
To la Nueva México.

The other side marks the site as the first
United States Geological Survey training center.
Established in 1888, those trained here made
Some of the earliest hydrological studies in the nation.
Hyper Nuevo, in an elaborate swirling turquoise graffiti script,
Is tagged over one of the corners of the sign.
It is someone's placaso and an affirmation of their presence.

Just like the countless petroglyphs throughout the valley,
They speak of the Indigenous peoples' presence and history,
Their comings and goings, their staying behind.
The cars on the highway whoosh past.
Folks eternally in migration and movement,
And there's no slowing down.
El tiempo, como Dios, se tarda pero no se le olvida.

II

Once, as a young man when I was hitchhiking through this canyon,
I was picked up by a hippie in a beat-up Ford Econoline van.
As we made our way through the winding two-lane road,
He remarked about how this place was starting to feel like home.
Hey, man, you know you can buy property anywhere out there, he said,
Crouched over the steering wheel like the Kokopelli dancer
Dangling from the rear-view mirror.

His long bony finger pointed out towards the plateaus and mesas.
I'm gonna get me a few acres and build a house.
I won't have electricity or water, but I'll be fine.
Through his dreamer's naiveté and enthusiasm,
I saw how a slight change in perspective
Can really put a hop in a person's skip.

Today, as I look across the gorge
toward La Cañada de Los Comanches,
I can see houses beginning to sprout like

Clumps of grass growing in the crevasses.
I wonder if one of those houses belongs
To that wandering gypsy hippie-dreamer.
Perhaps he too is looking out across the valley,
Gazing down from a precipice of a mountain.
Hay mas tiempo que vida, they say around here,
Knowing that life is limited but time goes on.

III

I was having a conversation with a childhood friend recently.
She was complaining about the younger generation.
She finds lack of manners upsetting and argues
For the need to teach good behavior and accept responsibility.
My friend laughs and places her hands on her hips.
She stands delicate but solid, like the sugar bowl on the table.

Sometimes I tell one of my nieces or nephews,
Go to the shed and get the rastrío, she says.
A what? They ask.
The rake. The rastrío.

They come back with the rastrío, and say,
Here you go, tía.
No, not for me. For you!
Rake up the leaves! I tell 'em.
¡Hijolé! These kids now 'days.

IV

We have morphed into our new shells.
Coyote tricksters never out of style,
But never quite current.
Defying time and space, static and mobile,
Like a trailer home set on cinder blocks without the wheels.

The tense, present and fleeting, always has us
Looking back to see how far we haven't gone.
It is a perfect union, like the cracks and creases of human skin.
That Texas bluesman had it right,
Time keeps on slippin', slippin', slippin',
Into the future.

There are life-accounts that will not be placed on a historical marker.
They are shaped from a poetry crudely composed, unstructured,
And versed, not through well-crafted literary devices,
But from stories that refuse to die even when the day's biggest news
Sounds like the *same ol', same ol'*.

La vida loca, that expressed chaos with unconnected lines
Woven together, always manages to skid its way in,
Like when the front tires catch a patch of black ice
And veer the truck onto the path of an oncoming vehicle.
El tiempo es presta'o, someone reminded me recently.
And it's true, we are living on borrowed time.

Monarch

Gregory L. (Goyo) Candela

for Sean Patrick Balassi

Quietly, I weep for the
Monarch butterfly.
I, an old man, cry
as this purposeful flutter, up
from Mexico, goes extinct.

My six-year-old
grandson studies bugs: he
recently, danced, around
and around, in my back
yard in Albuquerque
singing, "Bugs do what
they want to do, and bugs
go where they want to go."

In my summer childhood
I, too, danced—through the
wild oat fields of California's
Central Valley. Migrating
golden-orange sailors
shuttled among the sea
of sweet milkweed.

Now 80% of them are gone.
And my grandson looks up
at me and says, "Pa G, we
have to plant a lot of milkweed."

September Tomatoes

Tanesia R. Hale-Jones

The tomato slowly digested by the grasshoppers and fruit flies
A swarm ate one from the inside out
Entering along a split as the fruit cleaved itself
Against its own largess
Now a pale red skin, transparent, collecting dirt
The heat swells mid-day
I feel swallowed by it and try to think less as it consumes
Everywhere things are engorged
Spilling out and over
Mosquitos feast on my bare ankles in the evenings
I would be angry, but it feels too desperate for rage
And anyway, I am waterlogged and exhausted

The tomato has grown out and over the box
crushing the Ratibida columnifera and prairie daisies
nothing beneath the canopy reaches the sun, which seems like an impossibility
given the way the sun touches down with such vehemence
seems impossible that all of it is slipping off
The last push to produce
To bear fruit
To bloom brightly and with certainty
To expose your juice
To be devoured with such relish
I can hear the snacking from up close: to be so delicious
To be at the end and still eaten from the inside out
The glare of sunset
Asking us to remember that nothing is as it seems
All illusion and at last we get to watch it decay
With a kind of gluttonous extra
Eyeing the innumerable

Unendangered Weeds

Megan Baldrige

Hunkering survivalists bunker in my garden
flaunt, taunt, haunt me
as I walk the backyard.

Grab-hearted,
caliche-clinging foxtail grass
circles my house,

threatens take-over,
slices the hand that
weeds it.

Bindweed,
unapologetically
un-annihilated,

claims *my* dirt,
from its cave garden
under the sunflower roots.

Its tentacles choke
backyard rocks
in spools of roots,

chase hints
of water
into tight places.

Bindweed is here, and there,
and over here,
and over there.

It is born again every time
I dig up
a tiny sacrificial tendril,

then leave behind
the ancestral root
it sprang from.

Elm seeds warn me
"No vacation for you
this summer.

"You never know when the monsoons
will return to give us new life,
new life, new life, new life, new life, new life, new life.

"*We* never take a day off;
our sacred rite is to rule
your yard.

"We were here first,"
chorus the foxgrass,
the bindwind, the Russian thistle.

"Even if you rise at dawn
and come after us
with sharpened spades,

we never give up
our roots
our gnarled cojones, our underground brains."

Like a poodle
that dares howl at coyotes
I'm outgunned.

My coquettish
petunias
will not ruffle for long.

Yes, the bindweed
will wrap me
 in its arms

when I return to the garden someday—
as ashy dirt.

Unbridled

Janet St. John

Gate blown open, my mouth's
corral stocked with wild
four-legged words, the ones
that rush and gain traction
Oh, Listener, you on the receiving
end of dust, snorting, thunder,
my mane-shake attitude.
These hooves may stamp and
slam your ground. Shell-curve
edge, a blade that hides soft frog-
flesh within. I speak what I think,
feel, believe, without gentling
truths first. Now free
they stampede and trample
you, My Love, meek earth.

Swimming the Herd (How to Think Like a Cow)

Mary McCray

We spend our young life
mocking cows
and how they move like chaos,
plodding, milling, bawling stragglers.

The smell of shit, a dumb brute,
the dusty lunk-headed mob,
vacant, vapid heifers,
stubborn, mindless,
the ungovernable mass.

Their quiet unconcern as we count, recount
and tally our anxieties.

His thinker wouldn't make a teacup
for a hummingbird.

Nothing dumber than a cow,
except for the man that herds them;
it is the futility of a gnat
biting an iron bull.

At dusk they are the classic outline of balance,
centered into the earth.
Vaquero Joe sings Verdi's La Traviata
like a lullaby to the herd.
They gather bemused,
fleas buzzing above their humps.
Calm Brahmans, the long tongues
of Longhorns thickening.

They smell tomorrow's rain;
they side-eye your circling approach;
they stare at your audacity in disbelief,

chewing their cuds, re-digesting the facts
of each blade of grass
four times.
They know you lie.
They know you lie to yourself.

Mindless? Then they are what you seek,
your cattle koan to solve.
Listen to their low bellowing moo,
the Om of their meditation.
Enter the herd bovine.
Lay down on the plains
and dream of water.

I Walk Today Alone

Carolyn Fresquez

I walk today alone along the paths of Los Poblanos Open Space
a steady foot rhythm and whipping hair
a breeze on my face.

The mountains stand massive in the distance
nothing to obscure them
bottom to top
when you're on the West side.

And I imagine
sweetheart
you would kiss me under the golden light
the bright leaves of autumn honey-rich and shining.

The darkening sky to the North
a blueish grey rolling
whirling change so broad above the earth
holding the promise of snow, they say.
They say it'll be dry this winter. And they know.
They have a bird's eye view.

The air is still warm
this summer stretched 85 degrees into mid-October
but I can smell the edge of winter not-yet-here
conjuring the memory of every lonesome autumn
looking for you.

Brackish wind exchanging seasons
the sluggish heft of heat dispersed in a quickening current
lighting up the trees a shimmering fire
clattering their branches
rattling their leaves high above.

The grasses, too, have lost the soft whistle of green in the breeze
now paper rustling shudders
as the dust skips down the path
racing like a ghost about to take flight.

In my iterative imagination
I feel real only when I think of
what you might think of me
vulnerable to the belief amongst this expanse
that I am inconsequential.

And the cranes have to lift their long legs high
to step among the cut farm rows
they look at me the slightest bit wary
secure enough not to stop their business.

A road runner doesn't mind me either
scurrying a length of the pathway
by my side
forward and back
peeking for something to eat.

In the cracked mud of the acequias,
the sharp hand prints of a raccoon
I think
looking fast in its happy passage.

My own footprints and their moody impression
lost behind me in a dusty sea of many
many others
a busy path.

The ground is kiln dry
but there's the slightest rare bit of moisture in the air
carrying the smell of sweet plants and rich earth
from someone's house the smell of a church candle
until I pass a yard with a horse.

When I step inside our home every sense alight
you don't look up
though you ask me how it was.
I cannot say. My eyes have not adjusted yet.
Good, I say. I don't know.

My imagination fizzles
and I feel dispersed
like so many blowing leaves.

The Sandias, 2008

Olivia Gatwood

the only person who knows,
and i mean *really* knows—
from even eight states away,
a pitch so gentle only
he can hear it—my sadness,
is my father who, when i was sixteen
and experiencing my first heartbreak,
knew nothing but also
knew everything at once,
and without asking any questions,
took me on the back of his
motorcycle and drove us
up to the mountains where,
in the middle of summer,
we rode the ski lift
up and down, admiring, silently,
the tall grass and blond poppies
and untouched globes of dandelion
florets and the lonely boy
at his summer job who pulled
the lever just for us, the only
customers, to lift our bodies
up this silent beast, and i
was too young to point
and say, *how beautiful,*
still stuck in my teen religion
of black eyeliner, eyes rolling,
but knew, despite my denial,
that something here was
worthy of praise and i guess
that was the lesson,
my father, who knows,

and i mean *really* knows,
my sadness, knew that i
didn't need to be told,
i needed to see, that despite
it all, there was still
something alive beneath me.

from "What's not Atomic?"

V. B. Price

She was the best. She felt like shit,
Legs and back aching, memory ragged
Late at night, but she was game,
So game she goes on the road
Not quite clear all the time where she is
But always present, always kind, always
Gentle and forgiving, always open
To a symphony of birds
In weed trees near the tracks,
Malaise notwithstanding, malaise pains,
Malaise fatigue no motive power,
Only her generous and endearing will,
Her refusal to feel self-pity,
Keeping its saturation out
By a native and self-nurturing love
Of being alive, no matter the form
It's taking at the moment, no matter what,
she was loyal to love as it is.

To Be Alive in This City

Jessica Helen Lopez

for Burque

of magnetic undercurrents, magenta,
watermelon spilled light over the valley
of saltbush and scrub, wind-whipped
seasonal cruising of the tarmac,
jellyfish electric lowriders, Belair beauties
hydraulic horsepower of the V-8.

is to be alive and sucking in an arid
cold-desert air, lung-heat, and the surprise
party of the springtime wet monsoon,
sudden water dotting the brown earth.

is to be alive like an old ocean is alive,
ancient shell, sleepy volcano, pumice
of the heart.

The city says to me and I hear her:

Believe in medicina and in
the brujeria of the moon.

How she vibrates above
our thick-skinned skulls, sickle
cell, flat-white or golden-globule.

Leave your offering
at the altar of the foothill.
Take some dirt with you,
wash your feet, forehead,
nape and neck with its grit,
sand, and silt.

To be alive in this city means:

Repent
Pray
Protest
Love
Sweat

Covet the neon greens,
black of night, white-hot
star-riddled streakiness,
smeared *colores de agua*
of this brawling city,

night-time pusher and dealer,
empty-pocket bars and eight-balls,
sacred sex-workers and cigarette-smashed
suenos, hopeful bus rides
winding up and around
the hip bone
of downtown

then off, off, off you go
into the North Valley
of no snowfall.

Covet
Crawl
Crouch
Coo

To be alive in this city is to be alone.

Alone and bald and naked
as the day you were born,
swathed in a glowing,
sinful, sacred and slithering
phosphorescent light.

Part Three

Paths Cut Through the Dry Earth

In the Year of Our Peril

Sylvia Ramos Cruz

May 2020, Albuquerque, NM

In the year of our peril, my grandson Santiago turns sweet sixteen standing in his front yard watching a parade of ballooned cars bursting with family and friends (cornucopia of love in a rainbow of colors) wave and drop wrapped gifts on the sidewalk six feet away, no one ready, or even allowed, to hug him. Two fire trucks loud with Latin soul and salsa music—rhythms that dance in his Puerto Rican and African American blood—swing by. Firemen, on their way to lunch, stopping for a minute to bring joy to a young man on the threshold between what is and what will be his life in the world of adults.

it takes a village
when the lion comes
hungry

(a chorus hums)

In the year of our peril, one more unarmed Black man, George Floyd, a "gentle giant," is murdered by Minneapolis police in plain sight, inciting a string of protests joined round the world. People in all shades of light setting fire to the night with cries of JUSTICE, prompting 12-year-old Keedron Bryant to Instagram, "My people, we don't want trouble. Have had too many struggles. I just want to live."

chant of the ocean
icy and dark
lapping the shores of the heart
forever

(a chorus hums)

In the year of our peril, we walk el Bosque del Rio Grande, don and doff homemade cotton masks as we spy people on the trail, feeling frail as elders in this plague. Wonder why so many go unmasked. Venture their health and well-being, as well as ours. Behind us, the Hispanic Cultural Center holds the intonations of our ancestors whose words we no longer know— Taíno, Nahuatl, Yoruba, Tiwa, and hundreds more. We, multihued humans forged over five hundred years in the fires of Spanish colonization. Linked by a common language—lengua de los conquistadores. Español.

in nature
creatures speak in tongues
only they know

(a chorus hums)

In the year of our peril, we stop by a stand of white mulberry trees bowed by clusters of pink, red, purple fruit that taste tart like acerolas from our childhood backyard tree in Puerto Rico. Along a thread-like track lined with slender grasses, a man—ruddy-countenanced, sun, sand and sorrow seared—sits inside a grotto formed by a downed tree's branches. Legs crossed under, arms at sides, hands on lap. Face affect-less. Eyes lost to the river that was once high and mighty. The Buddha in meditation asks, "Do you have water?" Sadly, we have none.

so much water
he says
and no water

(a chorus hums)

In the year of our peril, we hear rat-a-tating as we leave the forest. Think, at first, it's a woodpecker pecking a new home. See, when the wind kicks up, a dead cottonwood swaying, singing (like abuela's creaky old rocker) its last words before falling unheard in the forest. Perhaps, the clamors rising in the red-eyed ashes from Minneapolis are the bugle call just before injustice falls.

tell me
what is the scent of rain
in the desert
for I have forgotten

(a chorus hums)

Pandemic Fatigue

Jenna L. Norton

A weight
a boulder, unmoved by white noise and cold coffee,
nestled in the winter-thick membrane
where a light used to be.
Little Libra,
unable or unwilling to accept another decade of the agony that is
(was)
your life.
As you leaned elbows on knees
in the hospital-approved and sanitized seat,
the only one with a comfortable cushion,
you announced what it was worth:
"I've got $11 in my bank account.
No one is here to save me."
When your body is a sieve,
words have no meaning.
They slip milk-white down the staircase into
that piece of you that deeply thinks you'll be alone forever
(even if this is untrue).
I wish we could return to it—a week ago.
I'd say what I couldn't and you wouldn't hear:
"it's not too late, we'll figure it out, you're going to move on."
But even I, saturated in degrees and hours of pain-mirrored postures,
know that isn't true for everyone.
It could not be true for you.
You've seen the ugly inside of this failing system.
The model was made
long before you gave yourself a choice.
You said there was no one left to mourn you,
that you'd keep one foot in this world.
"Who will feed my dogs?"
Even so,
I wonder about your pets.

They too must be feeling a sense of absence
where hope for you to get better
once was.
The windows cover an entire wall.
There exists a whirring of activity—neighbors walking.
I should be grateful for the view.
Instead,
envy rattles between my ribs,
a hollow rain stick of mostly human parts.
These strangers don't have to face another empty chair
in another empty hour
on another empty day
where you no longer exist.
And where I could not, as you predicted, save you.
Clouds spill over the foreshortened peaks;
the wind chills.
Observe.
Another storm rolls in.

prophesy on an Albuquerque day

Mary Oishi

a Diné poet/mother/multimedia artist told me today
that, according to the indigenous calendar,
we're about to leave what she calls "hell" cycles,
enter the cycles she and her people call "heaven"
when the Pleiades is directly overhead

"It will get worse before it gets better
but by 2038 the mixed people—and look at us,
we're all mixed—

the mixed people will take us back to
living with the earth again.

So says the prophesy," she said,
smiling down at her boy.

So says the prophesy, re-beats my weary heart,
weary of the cycles of pandemic hell, of
conspiracy hell, of
    mass shootings hell, of
       history-erasing hell,
          hell after hell—but
So says the prophesy.

So says the prophesy carries me like a refrain
glowing, warming my winter heart,
waiting for the mixed grandchild
who will bring heaven to earth for me this year
no matter where the Pleiades appears
on the night of her birth

perhaps she *will* help take us back,
perhaps by 2038 she and all the mixed peoples of earth
will usher in the "heaven" cycles.   At least—

So says the prophesy.

who am i to disbelieve?

Imagine Mars

Mary McCray

Imagine your life in a glass box,
cold, clean streets and the porcupine feeling
of antiseptic air.
Imagine holy days of rain,
a cyclone, staged burlesque
in a carnival.
Organized animal love.
Imagine everything Mars,
a world without squalling,
the gauzy breeze tribesmen tell of
in Legend of the Faucet Sky.
Imagine the smell of autumn in a test tube,
cloning sickly trees,
sheet-snapped flurries with nowhere to go,
leaflessness.

Veterano Sanctuary

Carlos Contreras

Puro Duranes.
Dirt and acequias behind the house
too much land to know what to do with
the best problem to have
in a city swallowed by concrete.

Soy de Rio Grande

Territorial stomping grounds
for people from
all colors on the palette.
Black, White, Brown.
Puro
Nuevo Mexicanos
Todos somos

Burnt brown or already there.
I am already here.
Son of the sun,
child of the earth,
screaming my existence at the clouds.

Maybe it will rain
one of these summer days
spent dirtying jeans
and callousing hands,
learning to me a man
the only way my father knew how
to teach us.

Sweat like braille.
Read the salt lines.

Read the hieroglyphics
Skin deep.
India ink, tattoos,
Dickies and Ben Davis.
Mad Dogs
and Mad Dog 20/20.
Boones Farm at 14.

Living the dream.

Dying slowly and smiling.
Slow-burning butts
of cigarettes in an ashtray.
Old Monte without an air conditioner
and good tunes.

Sunday afternoon
fishbowl cruise
no tint on the windows.
My City.

Definitely not
Worried about you, me,
Or anyone else,
She's self-motivated.

Seldom motivated to do anything
Before tomorrow, next week,
Next Wednesday.
But on Sunday nights
She shines like a Triple Gold Sunflower
100-spoke sunset.

Veterano Sanctuary
Isleta
Rio Bravo
Barelas Duranes
y todo.

Soy de ti
y el otro.
Todos somos
locos.

Coyotes
howling.
Full moon,
half-crazy.

Paint job
sun-baked,
half faded
summer nights
leave us half-faded.
Ay que Burque!
She's one crazy lady!
Princess puppeteer
stiff shot
Marlboro Light 100 in her clutches
and a cold beer.
Easy to please.

Easy breezy beautiful
Loca Girl
Lowrider songstress
Cheap-ass in the most
Expensive prom dress,
Todavía on a cruise,
that's a promise.

One she can keep.
No crossed fingers behind the back.
Just a whisper in your ear
and a lick down the length of your neck.
Cross your heart and hope to die
in a land enveloped in

Mountains, sun
sweat and dirt.
Mariachis, chile
and quinceañeras.
Chicharrones, margaritas
and pachucos.
Somos locos
hay todos
todos somos

Burnt brown or already there
I'm already here,
waiting for the sunset.

Hilltop

Tani Arness

When you arrive, I want to take you to the hilltop at night
and point out the kite and the scorpion.

My ability to be with you
depends on the stars and my ability to communicate with them,

my ability to soften into pattern and drift.
Sometimes I get so scared I can't even see God hovering

over the face of the dark waters.
I move from stardust to body and

sometimes I still cannot fathom what love is.
It is not always obvious that starlight is enough

but when we walk to the hilltop, to the reach of this galaxy,
I know that we actually exist here:

wind, dark and light, your hand in my hand,
a hovering over the face of the Nothing.

The problem is no one is what we dreamed we would be.
The problem is when I try to force things, they break.

It takes so much patience to act from peace.
We have to give so much to sit and stare into sky.

When you arrive, I will take you to the hilltop at night.

Hyder Park

Feroza Jussawalla

I came from Hyderabad to be healed,
at a park named after Hyders, lions, giants. The emperor who
founded my home town, Hyder-abad, was
a lion in his own right, from whom sprang
a long line of Nizams, rulers who embodied wealth.
This Hyder, here, a gentle Syrian immigrant named al-Latif
after the gentle form of the lion-shaped Allah, *"Haidrah,"*
of Hyderbad and Hyder Park. He, who must've generously
donated land he owned around Amherst street.

I came with breast cancer in 2001, drawn to a house
on Hyder street. It recalled my home, a Muslim town,
Hyderabad, though I am a Zoroastrian Parsi.
I came from the south, Las Cruces, the city of crosses,
when told that the Cancer Center in Albuquerque
could heal me. And though it did, it was the park.
In the middle stood a tree I hugged daily
on my prescribed walk. The bark, peeled back,
in the shape of a shaman, a healer, a doctor.
He sat there, carved by wind and weather
at the bottom of the tree and waited patiently for me.

My tree shaman sits on indigenous land: Pueblo? Navajo?
I thank him, for the land I enjoy, now, soft green turf
between my toes, the squishy earth between the roots, and
cottonwood leaves that oxygenate my cells. Healer.
This land, owned, as much as it can be owned by anyone,
Was once owned, by one separated from his indigenous land,
uprooted from Syria, rooted here—like I was,
uprooted from Persia, and India, evicted by war and politics.
But here we are, unhomed, homed.
Healed on the lands of all our ancestors, one people,
coming from all directions, to fill this vast diaspora.
Diaspora people, all.

Ditches

Tani Arness

My father knew the importance of using a shovel correctly.
He believed his rewards would follow the work of his hands.

He'd grab a shovel and show you how it's done,
the ways around the hard-packed clay and stones, the roots that must be cut.

My father was not one to give anything away easily.
He dug ditches for 400 years, working the long, hard hours of daylight.

I have inherited the deep lines he set,
have learned from the calloused hands of a ditch digger doing whatever it takes,

head bent over shovel, dried sweat on the brow,
sun on the back, and there's something like comfort there.

We want paths to be cut through the dry earth, we want water,
and we can grab, but we cannot own such things.

My father never waited for anything, not for God, or rain.
He jumped into it, digging, scraping metal against earth.

He knew how to dig a ditch deep enough to spill the water out like a song sung.
No, it didn't mean he was happy or generous, but there was something lasting,

maybe even something holy, in the shadows his laboring body cast across the land.

Almost Blue

Don McIver

for Chet Baker

I didn't even spot it until it moved
and it swept across my vision;
its wings a slow beating *whoop, whoop.*
Then it landed, across the shallow channel
from the one time island
that lets me walk to the middle of the *Rio*
without having to get my feet wet at all.
It stood and arched its back
and its wings were grey, almost blue.

Almost blue.
Its color, and the noting it in my head,
and I thought of Chet Baker
his missing teeth,
and how I almost lost mine too
when drunk,
I wrecked my bike
and flipped over the handlebars
and met the pavement.
Bits of teeth now replaced by some sort of dental cement.
I was more mad than sad,
more red than almost blue.

Almost blue.
The sky this morning is clearly blue
and the light plays tricks
as I can never really see the *Yerba Mansa*
and it's green leaves turning red
as fall moves slowly down the *Rio.*
The *Great Blue Heron* stood erect,

peering at me and perhaps wondered as I walked up towards him.
Am I a thing it should be bothered by
or is the sprightly, gangly black dog
that bounded in the water,
snapping at it to get its fill, the real threat?
The sky reflected in the muddy *Rio* is almost blue.

La Luz

Margaret Randall

The day I reached the top, a lifetime of sitting
burned the muscles of my calves.
I looked out beyond the city,
beyond the western mesa to extinct volcanoes
—line of dusky nipples tweaking horizon—
beyond Mount Taylor wrapped in Navajo prayer,
all the way to California.

Four thousand feet of switchback trail, eight miles
from desert to forested crest,
I needed a year and a half to advance by increments
through dry terrain of lower altitudes
past the turn where mountain stream
runs wet and dry and wet again
up to The Thumb

where two climbers we'd watched in their harnesses
died on the six o'clock news—how close
to our fascination, how briefly imprinted on our lives—
into the cooler upper mountain air,
back and forth across the rock slide
until the trail leveled off along knife's edge
through wooded highlands to the tram.

Sometimes we'd ride that tram up mountain
and hike down, others we'd start below
and make our slow way to the top.
Some days we'd round a bend in the trail
and startle a deer,
its deep brown eyes locked on ours,
its silence momentary trance.

Lizards and rabbits scurried from our step,
rattlers sunned themselves
on flat rocks or mid-trail.
Canyon wrens and peregrine falcons
offered their song
as we climbed farther, got higher,
accepted

the mountain's invitation to seasonal waterfalls,
a thousand bright blue butterflies
in one astonished cloud,
scrub cedar and piñon giving way
to oak and pine and ponderosa
as we lifted ourselves out of ordinary clutter
in twenty-first-century America.

Despite a childhood of forged gym notes
and couch potato lethargy
I kept that date I didn't know I had.
Cacophony of mountain sound
reduced in my ears to a single note
until the bird call or warning rattle
recognized themselves in me.

While it lasted, my mountain
taught me purpose and time,
answered any question.
Now that lungs fade
and muscle and sinew no longer do their work
I've learned to plant its memory
in the poem.

Chile Hearts

Crystal Coriz

You can't top a mountain as monstrous as a valley of land. Whose enchantment depends on the eyes of the believer. But you still remember the past, the beginning of development. Thoughtfulness slips through the grass as you try to laugh in the infection of your beauty, but your bright-casted shadow dimly shines above your out-reached eyes. And that's no lie. Acceptance, an important part of your life, from the spices, to the sugars any time, there is no limit to what you perceive. But do you know the meaning of losing flavor? Because of imagination, a body of water turns into a sea of lights, a ponder of being trapped in magic. You are my special, one and only special. Setting all these examples are static lights, as they empty there is always something new to do. Light up in advance. Switch. The looking glass is new, and the adventure is set downtown. Towards the accomplishments of development and self expression. You watch as the lighter layer of gray shifts off the land. It's eye, round and demanding, knowing that it's important to consider. You watch the lonely way birds fly with no avail. The irony being they have one set destination. It's considerate. A world's end evident in the drastic way we glorify rain. The night is nearly ending, rewinding the clock until the sun greets us again. Everything changes at the glow of dusk.

In Bernalillo, A Blessing

Jules Nyquist

> . . . if I stepped out of my body I would break
> Into blossom.
> —*JAMES WRIGHT*

In the palm of my hand
arrives spring
I stop the car for bursting wisteria
I can only take a photo
in the age of stay-at-home pandemic

I meet my friend in the parking lot
of Tractor Supply on 2nd
she is low on toilet paper
and I give her six rolls in a bag
in exchange for some flour

We smile with our eyes
she is wearing a mask in her car
I set the bag in her trunk
along with an Easter card

We won't be gathering for brunch this year
the road sign on the way down says
Stay Safe, Social Distance, Shop Alone
even the casinos are closed
the billboard with our beautiful mountain
says Flatten the Curve

Tractor Supply has baby chicks
but I don't go in
just drive the slow road home
traffic is light and no one is tailgating
or in a hurry

The cattle graze, horses are in the fields
and a guy with a cowboy hat
leads his horse out of the trailer
Someone put out a "Baby Goats" sign
and the cottonwoods are catching up in green

For this moment
I hold spring
in my palm
home is two of us and two cats
we're healthy
we know what's for dinner
we eat on our patio
we can hold hands

Misa

Michelle Otero

En vez de trompeta, garza
En vez de nave, claro
En vez de vía crucis, álamo, álamo, álamo
En vez de reclinatorio, arena
En vez de pila, río
En vez de coro, cigarra
En vez de cura, yo

Part Four

Strange Transformations

New Mexico Department of Tourism (A Haiku)

Hakim Bellamy

Albuquerque. Where
the desert doesn't get in
the way of your view.

Out West

Peter Pachak-Robie

Pistols were inked in their holsters, a luna moth
pinned to her back, there were also two pink scars,
both from her firebug phase, and a black cloth
riddled with holes she'd squint at and name stars
Xanadu, Eden, or Heaven 2. They were ours.
Seventeen, underpass-motel-high, we're stuck
right in a bleeding southwest sunset; our luck
written in rabbits' circadian footsteps thumping
out a vending machine's last pack of Golds.
Stereo starlight vibes—some kind of humping
prism of time with seven paths—unfold,
one to a golden west and six she'd been told
faded. I had to ask a friend at school
what she had meant by "copulate in a pool."

When the River Liked to Party

Megan Baldrige

Way back when the Rio Grande was a wily teen,
April-partying bosque bad boy,
every flood-year the rio grew double grande.

Way back when, the snow-swelled river
jumped its banks,
burst forth for a night out on the burque.

Way back when, the rushing, rollicking Rio Grande
bounded borders, basements, backyards,
enthusiastically infusing water into the valle.

Way back when, the flooding river
waved its muddy waters,
sowed the seeds of a new generation of cottonwoods.

Way back when, on such a weekend of ribald revelry,
seeds were borne to sandbars, a thirsty nursery was cradled in water;
a forest was reborn.

Way back when, the Rio Double Grande raced itself,
flaunting its flow on parched earth,
until retiring to meander.

Way back then, the life of the party left a legacy,
a litter of cottonwoods,
high-water hijinks saplings, the flood generation of 1942.

Nowadays, Cochiti Dam kiboshes.
A strict parent enforces a no-floods policy
for its wayward charge.

No more river malarkey:
birth control reigns in the bosque.

from "The Sandias, Spring 1972"

R. Naso

1. El Topo

We all crowded into Michael's old pickup
to see Alejandro Jodorowsky's film *El Topo*
at an art-house theater somewhere in the U
district, afterwards parsing it all night long
in a nearby student commune, drinking
and getting high, not returning until dawn.

Michael and his old lady lived in a two-room
adobe, the rest of us in one-room cabins
scattered along the west side of the highway.
Back then if I had passed by my present self
on East Central, I wouldn't have recognized
anything in common with him-me-us.

As I remember it now, this was a dominate
theme of Jodorowsky's movie–the strange
transformations that life undergoes in time
from god-like template to deformed victim
of the all-seeing Pharaonic-kapitalist dollar.

I never had more than a dollar and change
in my own pockets back then . . .

Like a flashing red light (which Duke City
motorists are more than likely to ignore)
those rare and sacred places where one
passes by oneself both coming and going—
Danger, proceed with caution, melancholy
alienation and extreme nostalgia likely.

Central Avenue

Bill O'Neill

Matching Hoppity as we survey Central Avenue one
half hour before noon,
the same broken families with their helpless
progeny finding the home of their street.

Hippity explains it to me, waving his hands as
he does; together we walk down the forlorn
avenue: motels, the cheap assessment of a day, or
what can be done amid Spandex & where appetites
reach their logical conclusion.

"Why bother?" I ask rhetorically: "The same people,
this endless stream that I see in the mirror of
my Volvo? People like us must need to feel
viable, I guess . . ."

And Hoppity, characteristically misunderstanding:
"No!" he exclaims. "That isn't true. It *does* make
A difference. Just ask our Hope House alumni—"

I could say a number of things at this point:

"Is Sam still on the avenue gunning his stolen
Dump truck?"

"Is the whole point simply to not bounce checks?"

"To be normal enough to safely navigate the mall?"

Or, "The avenue waits here every day for what washes
in the dry air of our longing."

Or, "What would my life have been without
this need to *improve* the surrounding world?"

But I say nothing.

"See?" Hippity continues in his not getting. "It
is undeniable. We *can* improve our lot!"

Okay. But it will always be there, as a man
slows down and detours around the block,
need that drives our being; she awaits on the street . . .

Or the cavernous movie theaters jammed, without
surprise, everything becoming

way too simple,

the beaming couples holding their newborns like collateral.

In a House on Candelaria Road

Ryan M. Stark

for Jim Morrison

There is wonderworking here
for the ghost tourists.

They seek a revelation,
genuflecting, murmuring
their *Densmorekriegermanzarekmorrison*
mantras.

They seek a vivid manifestation,
like the sky spreading its thighs
to serve their imaginings.
As if Jim, in five-year-old form,
was crowned the Lizard King right here.

They seek mercy
from the whirlwind of smoky years
in a way that brings the man to them now,
wearing chains
in some extra-dimensional Ed Sullivan moment.

And they seek retribution
against the Paris bathtub-deathbed itself,
ululating,
like the fans of some minor gladiator
on the wrong end of the sovereign's thumb.

All Eyeteeth out of the Cocoon

Susan Mitchell

Whatever is dually
Warned,
Soberly returns,
To procure
Knock-about live-wires,
The kind of love that sticks
To your ribs,
And spits you back out,
Half the touch,
Followed to the letter.
It's always amateur
Until another anti-christ
Cries everyone's game.

In this world
Trust was nothing more
Than want,
Nothing more than a
New cut of meat,
Delicate clamorings over
Nothing
Splitting the chests of narrow men,
Blood falling onto newly washed plates,
And silver from someone's
Mother's Wedding
And cups left empty of that desire.

Want is a fearful thing
When it breaks or bursts
Suddenly,
Without any breather or respite,
With heart in mouth precious,

Press the damn reservoir,
Dusty with parrot patron saints
To widows, orphans, handymen,
Cabaret singers, poker players and
Rotting fruit
Falling out of unpaid
Taxicab doors.
Whatever pulls the lamp light
Is curling, kinking, untying,
Loosening the guillotine.

It's always about the wrong horse,
Falling down a flight of stairs,
Waiting with the body until dawn
Dissolving in Oaxacan leather.

The biggest mistakes
Are like the legendary
Child-Scarer,
All eyeteeth out of the cocoon,
Screaming thick lipped garbage
With a ballpoint pen
About a kiddish prod,
Aficionados becoming huge in
A sour game of chess.

If nothing else,
Remember this.
Drown it out.
Drooling like a cartoon dog.
Maybe it's about time to sit down and cry
Wishing with a single sole
You could crush
Law and Order,
Dominance and convenience stores,
Addiction and Lucky Filters.

Searching for Crowns in a Pile of Two by Fours

Zachary Kluckman

It's the same everywhere.

The new guy gets the shit
work, ain't hard—just tedious.
Like all you got hands for is splinters.
but if you can't cut roof
or nail a tee together they stand
you next to a pile of two by fours
tell you to inspect the wood.

A man with the right frame
of mind might find it fun. Remember
all the days spent poking dead
things with sticks, how perfect
the wood had to be for your
rubber band bows and arrows.

Now it's sweat equity and labor.
A morning spent moving wood from one
pile to another, like it won't all
get used anyway. Like all of you,
with your sunburnt faces, won't
all get used up anyway.

But there's a simple beauty
to the search; getting lost in the
scream of saws, the dull thud of nails

finding home, the laughter of
men and women who know what honest
work means, what calloused hands
mean to a family.

The wood has to be just so
or has no integrity. Won't hold
a nail or a family proper, so you caress
the wood with your eye. A twist
in the grain will warp a whole wall,
but the ones that arch like your wife's
eyebrow when you tell a dirty joke,
you call them crowns.

Imperfection means the wood
didn't dry right, means point it all
the same direction or pay hell
when you drywall. Maybe you begin
to believe this is a kind of art.
Puzzle piece the wood, joke

as if your hands are doing
the most important work in the yard,
shit, can't have crowns in my wood.
Ain't no royalty around here, son.

It's the same everywhere.

Always the poor man building
the rich man's house
with the best wood he can find.
Every time you cash that check
you think how the poor man has to have
a steady hand, trying to build a life

from another man's wood, how
the rich man stacks his cash like a pile of
two by fours, how the ones
with all the crowns

can bring the whole house down.

Morning Blessing

Mark Fleisher

Nestled under the rush
of streaming interstate traffic
Coronado Park's green oasis
disgorges the night's residents
who huddle against the chill
of an Albuquerque drizzle
as they shuffle down Third Street
bent over from bearing
a burden of modest treasures,
well-worn backpacks, bedrolls,
blankets, indescribables crammed
into a shopping cart long absent
from its supermarket corral.

Homeless steering themselves
to St. Martin's welcoming door
for a daily shot of hope and faith
before claiming a favored street corner
seeking generosity from passing strangers,
later recycling into eerie darkness.

All the while from wherever
saints gather the holy man
looks lovingly upon seekers
of his grace, his cloaked arms
uplifted, devoutly blessing all
for Martin is the patron of beggars.

Albuquerque, 2nd and Lead

Tina Carlson

Live, say her markers, and she makes a sign.
In her pack, a knife to soothe the child she was,

whose codes she misunderstands. Order and slack.
She is a poem, scrawled on a drum. Scavenges

face masks, hairbrush, pop cans. She tries to feel
worthwhile. A man tosses pennies, she splinters

her feet. Bleeds her arms, sap from the trees.
Brother me, the man says in her mouth.

Cut, say her arms, *we exist*. She looks for a thin branch
to shred with her teeth. *Leave me alone*, says her tongue.

In a pocket torn from a girl's flowered dress, she harbors
a cross. Inside, all spring and hopefulness. *Stay* says her stomach

rattling like a train. Ask for a dollar, they all speed away. She
tears at the night. All those stars winking, as if in on a joke.

Late Night 66

Anna C. Martínez

Saunter by the window of a well-lit joint after a long long dizzying university day
glimpse feta crumbles on crisp spinach salad
carafe of red wine
they dine at a table for two with a checkerboard cloth
holding eyes across settings as you dart your own
because you've just a dollar for bus fare and
reflection betrays your hunger
Stop
wait beside the spilling trash outside a new window
a bar that fixes shrimp platters for warm democrats
who stir and sip margaritas
crunch on ice and savor coarse salt from the rim
you turn away and hell no
dude must think you've a backpack bag of tricks
way he licks his lips
whistles each time he circles the block in his cancered pick-up truck
so you walk slowly on past and step over the shoes of
lives being sucked inside glass bottles
disguised as brown paper bags
like the tricks being turned by a twig of a girl
maybe eighteen
stumbles onto Central from an unlit alley
pants undone
eyes glazed
sunken mouth
bare feet
offering fun to everyone she meets
taken by the driver of a blue minivan through a sliding back door
baby seat in the back
erase that if you can
Outrun the bus to the next stop and get on at last
hope that stinky ass don't sit by you
in greasy Levis he's slept and sweated
smoked stroked petted and scratched his balls in all-week-long

glad to see instead you get a skinny dude
in a self-proclaimed righteous mood
tells a friend his twenty-first birthday is Friday and
all he really needs to set himself free are
two fat chicks and a fat green stash and
you turn his way and try not to laugh and
take home hope for the world from wherever you can
'cause damn
tonight it's ramen for dinner again.

Albuquerque Past, Present, and Future

Elaine Carson Montague

Red-cloaked *Sandia* Mountains
Reflect K-spar crystals
Embedded within granite
Landscape thrust high, tossed wide
By antiquity's tongues of magma
Volcanoes dormant on the horizon
Near petroglyphs with messages
Silent as paw prints
What clues will I leave for future residents?
Love for the Albuquerque valley,
And its water supply?
An ache to be wrapped in the watermelon cloak?

Vibrant yellow-pink-purple and
Orange-sliced sunrises and sunsets
Kindle my soul
With promises for vigorous life and
Renewal in sweet repose
My heart beats to drumbeats near tracks
Of covered wagons and rails that brought settlers
With aromatic lavender to join
Indigenous ones in open spaces
The *rio* that feeds the bosque's ribbon of green
Sometimes barely a trickle
Welcomes colorful chutes atop gondolas of gold

Burque Neighbors

Rene Mullen

Lattice streets and wafting fire-roasted green chile connect
us, where Christmas is red and green and piñon blankets
the city in fireside dreams. Here we burn
to better ourselves and our community—chile, sage, Zozobra.
The only place in America where Route 66 collides
with Route 66, where balloons invade sunrises,
backyards, where ART divides north and south,
murals go this way, poetry goes that way and that way and
tourists flock to turquoise jewelers from greener
spaces, always asking, Why is it so brown?
So many neighborhoods, so many shadows, the oldest
buildings are shackled by the past, their choices
and those taken. This New Mexico whiptail sheds its enchantment
in order to plunder its land of—the gated call it violent,
those without, know otherwise—in a poor community, a castle
made of diamonds and gold stands at attention as proof
sacrificing eyes and ears makes for silent screams as sunsets
harvest the smoke, hear the echoes, turn it breathtaking, turn it magic.

The Sounds of Albuquerque's Heart

Jeff Sims

are of earth colored
grass and the cloudless wind.

Honey flavored shadows
and monsoon flowers.

A ballet of balloons
brushed upon sunrise.

Falling leaves between
fingers of praying trees.

An emerald smear
and water fear.

Skin the sun
has turned to scales.

Melon mountains that
rise from an empty sea.

The sometimes snow spread
between unsettled streets.

Concrete scrawl
and suburban sprawl.

A summer sun that
sings of the little things.

Sacred sunset sudden
close to another day.

Grandma's Last Cruise

Damien Flores

The day of her funeral, Grandma shut down traffic on Central Avenue for one last time. The hearse drove up 8th street and we took the roundabout on the way to San Felipe; we made all Downtown late for work.

I stared out the window of the Bereaved's Limo, as we followed Grandma for one more cruise down her favorite streets. Route 66 twists and winds like the arroyos and acequias in our neighborhood, like veins and arteries, like cottonwood roots.

Burque's street-people were always in her prayers. Pobrecitos, they don't have nobody to take care of them, she would say—give a pocketful of change, or a dollar if she could spare, when we passed them, but a prayer, always—*Mi Tata Dios takes care of us all, even when we don't know it. Give them a place to sleep tonight, something to eat. Tata Dios, take care of them.*

Along the way, I caught a glimpse of the people standing at the curbs and bus stops. Every person on Route 66 stopped and bowed their heads that morning as she rolled by, real slow. Grandma never liked to drive fast.

A little viejito on the corner of San Pasqual Street lowered his cycs until we passed. He wasn't the only one.

Los Pobrecitos of Central Avenue were the army of saints and angels who welcomed Grandma home. All paid their respects with quiet tears. Maybe reminded of their own dead-and-gone, some blessed themselves and slowed their hustle down, for a moment. Grandma shut Central down!

You should've seen it!

Some drivers, parked at the green lights, turned off their stereos. One woman glared at us. She would have made it to work on time if it hadn't been this particular day, when a hearse-plus-fifty-cars strolled through the intersection at 14th Street.

When we cruised through Old Town, we took the long way around. Just a few weeks before, the Plaza was a summer-bloom of music and laughter, even San Felipe himself leapt from his altar and danced when the church was empty. But today, his church was full.

Everyone was there. Shame the only time we all get together is when someone dies.

This time, Rosella H. Perez was the saint we prayed to.

Grandma out-lived all the other priests, so the new Father didn't know her. Before the service, he asked my favorite memory. I told him, I'll remember driving around with her. I'll remember for as long as I live.

During his Homily, Father contemplated heaven, how when we cross the gates, we are young again. All our pains and afflictions cured. I even took communion that day, even though I wasn't supposed to because he who is without sin cast the first jeño.

After the funeral, we cruised Mountain Road to Calvary Cemetery. The same road we drove everyday when she'd take me to school. I remember those years. Some days, it was real hard to go to Albuquerque High, knowing my whole family was dead and buried right across the street; knowing someday, I'd end up there too.

This time, we got to run all the red lights, 'cuz we had The Law on our side, we paid that little extra for the Police Escort.

Auntie Teri realized from the front seat, *Don't you think Mom would've liked this last cruise?*

That moment, I looked at my family, all stoic like saints, all caught in their own memories.

At the cemetery, we said our goodbyes with roses in her grave. Just before we lowered our Grandma in that holy dirt, Cousin Sylvia played Grandma's favorite song,

Con la Tierra Encima: Cuando yo me muera, no quiero que lloren hagan una fiesta con cuetes y flores.

And I couldn't help but remember, the car radio tuned to 89.1 as I took her for some long, good cruises around town; the last couple years I spent with Grandma; how she wouldn't leave the house if she had it her way, but I'd talk her out of it.

Let's go get lost for a while, I'd tell her, all the times we didn't have money but we had a full tank of gas, and that's all we needed.

I remembered the two of us taking the old road to Santuario, making visits to the Barrio Churches on Holy Thursday, driving up West Central to grab a banana split. Grandma's stories, so detailed you would've never known her memory wasn't what it used to be. Albuquerque sure has changed, she'd say at every turn.

Our lives are a cruise down a broken highway. Sometimes a dirt road, sometimes paved in gold; some race to their deaths, some take it easy, and don't get too far before their dead end. Some cruise real slow, and take in all the sights before the gas tank runs empty.

Today, one year later, Central Avenue is all torn down. The road is broken open like a half-dug-grave; like a robbed tomb.

But Today, her favorite song just came on the radio and I know she is here. Grandma sits beside me as we're stuck in downtown traffic. And as we finally catch the green light at Rio Grande Boulevard, I hear her say,

We ain't in no hurry anyways. Let's just enjoy this long drive home, one last time.

Part Five

EKCO

Excerpt from "Burque O Burque: Atom and Eva," an EKCO Collaboration

Maiyah King, Valerie Martínez, Michelle Otero, Monica Sánchez
first performed for the United States Department of Arts and Culture (USDAC)
Culture/Shift Conference, November 1–3, 2018, Albuquerque

I. From the Foothills, This

Four poets/voices,
Four music stands, tree branches with leaves, soundmakers, stones

ALL:
From the foothills, this—

ONE:
—place of sanctity.

TWO:
On the first day, god made the kitchen—

THREE:
—gathered flames from a distorted guitar—

FOUR:
—gathered city lights to the ruffles
on her broomstick skirt.

ONE:
She cut the ice-cold Sandia into small pieces—
into us, her children, one-hundred percent
green chile dreams—

ALL:
Burque!

Shaking leaves, soundmakers

TWO:
Sunrise eyes—

THREE:
—reveal our ancestors' fingertips
on petroglyphs.

FOUR:
The horizon is a channel widening
between clouds and sky.

ALL:
A thunderstorm!

Tap stones rhythmically

ONE:
The way black enters from the north
and veers right under cloud heft.

TWO and FOUR:
Burque!

THREE:
Going in curves and circles,
Always spinning out.

FOUR:
Every morning, from the foothills,
the ansisters' pulse shimmers
and glimmers down.

TWO:
Burque is small—

THREE:
—creation inside a giant horizon—

ONE:
—more sky than city—

TWO and FOUR:
—turning, shifting—

THREE:
—cruising low and slow,
roaming the war zone on Central.

ONE:
City of misperceptions,
are you shifting?

ALL:
Tectonic plates in loud crashes.

THREE:
City of underground melodies.

FOUR:
Burque calls, echoing to the valley—

TWO:
—together with elemental allies—

THREE:
—the little ones, our ancestors—

ONE:
Orishas—

FOUR:
Orishas—

TWO:
Orishas.

ALL:
We dance.

XI. Blue Enormous Bird

THREE:
Where are you, Albuquerque?

ONE, TWO, and FOUR:
Are you singing scorching Saturday
and Sunday mornings?
Are you the bosque
feeding this blue, enormous bird?

THREE:
Are you the way it bends?

ONE, TWO, and FOUR:
We drive the city, stare up
in amazement, even if it means
light in the land of the atomic bomb.

THREE:
Atom and Eva.

ONE, TWO, and FOUR:
Are you singing scorching Saturday
and Sunday mornings?

THREE:
Cottonwood drifting like goose down.

ONE, TWO, and FOUR:
Posole in the morning,
red chile, eggs and beans,
beating our drum song
of resilience.

THREE:
How do I show you—

ONE, TWO, and FOUR:
Eva, Atom—

THREE:
—this place we are from.

ALL:
Where you have to learn
the language of revolution.

Shake leaves, soundmakers

XII. Cicada Chorus

Call and response with audience

POETS:
Just say the names—

ONE:
—a cicada chorus.

POETS:
Tiguex. *(invite audience)*

AUDIENCE:
Tiguex.

POETS:
El Super. *(invite audience)*

AUDIENCE:
El Super.

POETS:
West Mesa women. *(invite audience)*

AUDIENCE:
West Mesa Women.

POETS:
Sandia man. *(invite audience)*

AUDIENCE:
Sandia Man.

POETS:
Atom. *(invite audience)*

AUDIENCE:
Atom.

POETS:
and Eva—*(invite audience)*

AUDIENCE:
and Eva.

POETS:
Stratocumulus snowpeak butte grassland plain. *(invite audience)*

AUDIENCE:
Stratocumulus snowpeak butte grassland plain.

POETS:
Snake. Stone. Song. *(invite audience)*

AUDIENCE:
Snake. Stone. Song.

POETS:
The frontier. *(invite audience)*

AUDIENCE:
The frontier.

POETS:
Mud. *(invite audience)*

AUDIENCE:
Mud.

POETS:
Heart. *(invite audience)*

AUDIENCE:
Heart.

POETS:
Burque. *(invite audience)*

AUDIENCE:
Burque.

TWO:
Somos luz.

FOUR:
Somos agua.

TWO:
Be something.

THREE:
Be someone—

FOUR:
—in a land that doesn't know the word—

POETS:
—easy—

FOUR:
—but knows a haunting well.

TWO and THREE:
Sacred, angry, calm.

ONE and FOUR:
Fierce, strategic, loving.

POETS:
Somebody, the some bodies we can be and be, here.

Excerpt from "Anyway, We Live," an EKCO Collaboration

Valerie Martínez, Michelle Otero, Shelle VanEtten de Sánchez
first performed in March 2015 as part of "Women and Creativity," a month-long series of events celebrating Women's History Month. The poem responds to twenty-two "containers" (bags, bottles, boxes, books—metal, ceramic, fabric, wood, glass) and their stories contributed by women who live in Albuquerque

V. "All These Grandfathers"

Three poets/voices. Poets at music stands.
Conversational.
Manly, Earthy.

ALL:
All these grandfathers:

ONE:
veteranos, fishermen, woodworkers,
penitentes, santeros.

TWO:
Grandpa lived on a little dirt road
between Menaul and Alameda—
A road well traveled by me
and everyone in my family.

THREE:
He was the King of Silky White Hair.

TWO:
Overalls held him for some part of every day
and probably the previous four decades
except when he danced.

ONE:
He was a special customer at the bar on North 4th.
He gave me a blue velvet bag that read:
Crown Royal.

Playful

THREE:
We laughed loudly—granddaughter and grandfather—
Willy One and Willy Two,
with our big fake mustaches
and shrinking eyebrows, sideburns
coming on and off each hour.

Sage. Story.

ONE:
Grandpa said: *Once upon a time there was a river—*
blue, wide, free. The animals came to its banks to drink.
The birds fluttered across its surface looking for food.
Rocks found a home. Leaves drifted and stayed.
Tree branches sunk, wistful, into her deep.
The first hunters gathered, thirsty, where she roamed.
Farmers took water for their fields, and prayed in honor.
Then, as it happens, more people came.
They had their needs and distractions.
Streets, homes, dams. More water left.
More and more. The farms disappeared.
The river emptied and dried.

ALL:
Everyone is looking for water.

Poets shift positions. "Looking."

THREE:
It wasn't until he died
that they talked about it.

I wasn't there for the wreckage.
I snatched hurts and injuries
as they floated through the air.

TWO:
He said: *open your eyes wide,*
now your mouth. Now lay your palms
flat on the table. Pray to the walls
and floors of mud, to the fields,
to the old pinto beans now sprung
with buds. Make a paste from two powders
and smear it on the back of your ears.

ONE:
He said:

ALL:
I'll be proud of the woman you'll become.

THREE:
I poured it in, all of it, a stream of hope,
a layer of wishing. Snow in the mountains,
spring-melt carving the long blue ribbon,
that stretch of road.

Discovering.

TWO:
I find the box, I find the letter holder,
pen holes, I find the postmarks, 1935,
5-cent stamp, expertly placed
by Grandfather's aging hands.

ONE:
Wood box with a tin latch; ceramic vase
that looks like Mother River.
I walk the river, fill the vessel at 11,000 feet
and carry it with me.

TWO:
So many containers, so many prayers,
memories, hurts and stories.

Layered and repeated.

ALL:
Words mixed with paper
Silver hoop
Teardrop of spring-green thumb
Beads the colors of sunset
One pearl
Black feather with green polka dots
Purple bow
Blue glass

Bold and wistful.

ONE:
At night, the old blue river rises up, coughs,
sings in my grandfather's gravelly voice:

ALL:
Water, glass, mud, bones, need,
are we.

Excerpt from "A River Runs Through Us," an EKCO Collaboration

Jasmine Sena Cuffee, Jamie Figueroa, Valerie Martínez, Shelle VanEtten De Sánchez

first performed in the Rio Grande riverbed, 2013

PROLOGUE

> *Four poets/voices. Poets stand side-by-side.*
> *One holds a pitcher, then pours a drop into the mouth of the poet to her right,*
> *and then pours a drop into her own hand. She hands the pitcher*
> *to the next poet. Repeat, repeat, repeat.*

ONE:
A drip.
This one is for you,
    this one is for me.

TWO:
A drop.
This one is for you,
    this one is for me.

THREE:
A wish.
This one is for you,
    this one is for me.

FOUR:
A story.
This one is for you,
    this one is for me.

PART TWO

Poets gather around table with river rocks,
collect them, pass, and put them back.

TWO:
In a family of secret-keepers
gathering stories can be a difficult task.
Wet mother, grandmother and all of her mothers,
did they not tell you how to make the river speak?

THREE:
They talked about the Greeks and the river of the dead.
We know deep in our feet that we must have respect,
listen for crashing waves, the wind song of flash floods—
carry coins in our pockets just in case.

ONE:
We became pilgrims retracing the steps of our ancestors,
learned that if we walked long enough,
we'd reach whatever was pulling us.

THREE:
We'd walk hand in hand and convince ourselves
we were warriors of the water.
We'd walk until there was no more concrete—

FOUR:
—to the places where the land gives way to movement,
water sculpting a body into curves, depressions,
hills and mountains.

TWO:
If you want to become better at anything,
you must sit by the river and listen—

FOUR:
—to the song the rivers give to the soil,

mute in itself, music when it loosens
and joins the running water.

THREE:
Rio del Norte, Rio Bravo, Rio Grande.

ONE:
You chase the blue sky south forever, smell the rain before it comes.

TWO:
Our veins resemble the windings of the Rio Grande.

FOUR:
They say this is how the world reveals itself.
They say it like we have been told a secret
and this is the only way they can share it.

THREE:
Make a wish, a song.

ONE:
This is your private bone and just as dry, just as hollow.

FOUR:
If you can fight through the suffering,
the rippling of the river becomes clear.
The heart slows itself and the eyes open again
for the first time.

ONE:
The Sandias tumbling north toward the Sangres,
the place where Rio Grande meets the Santa Fe
at Cochiti—confluence of wet river and dry.
The contrast, the continuance, the seam—

THREE:
—watching her swell, thin, drift—lapping
the tongues of cow, horse, bear, coyote—

TWO:
—through gills, over scales and open eyes,
under foot, under log and board and bridge—

FOUR:
—under gaze, under canoe,
under swollen yellow plastic—

ONE:
—slipping between shoots and sprigs,
through meadows, deserts, dams—

THREE:
—Falcon, Amistad, Anzalduas—

FOUR:
—into reservoirs and man-made lakes,
through cities, by maquiladoras, migrant workers,
remnants of vineyards, wheat fields and burial grounds—

TWO:
—buoying the dreaming bodies of earth.

THREE:
—and gathering, and swelling, and rushing relentless,
overflowing, making things lean, making things list—
trailer home, phone booth, swing set—

ONE:
—pulling down corn stalks and stop signs, cottonwoods,
tearing everything from their sinewy roots—

FOUR:
—then slowing, dwindling, almost vanishing
into the white hot, then trickling and threading,
winding its way—

THREE:
—under wing: butterfly, firefly, dragonfly shimmering—

FOUR:
—under sun, under orange-moon—

TWO:
—noise of waves, sheen of sand—

THREE:
—untouched, untamed—

ONE:
—the sound of earth's creatures waking.

Video: text of audience refrain, below.

AUDIENCE:
Pray to be covered.
Pray to float.
Pray to be carried.

Part Six

Sky Kingdom

Sijo for the Albuquerque Seasons

Scott Wiggerman

Fragrant fall, when cottonwoods release colors, cushion the earth
in leavings, a sweet perfume with every step in the forest,
food for worms in the detritus—how we forget death below.

*

Stiff winter, cold without snow, in windy skies a single flake,
white and sheer, light and lonely, like a whisper with a mission,
a brief life before it departs, so delicate, radiant.

*

Rainless spring, tempest of dust in from the west, dark walls of winds
pouring in—hear the whistle through the branches, a mocking scratch
dry as sand that lodges in throats, no oases, just sere tease.

*

Soft summer, the gentle hints of sweet breezes, honeysuckle,
and strangers open to love or sacrifice, to blossoming
into arms like constellations, laden with scents too soon spent.

Ritual

Alissa Simon

I

Wild rhubarb
    ready to redden
tall as rabbit ears, tucked
    in pockets
of sandy arroyo bed.

I face west, sunrise
    at my back
volcanoes in the distance. One
    lonely jackrabbit
silently sprints to safety.

I live between a volcano and
    the edge
of two tectonic plates, musical
    peaks which
rise, like the sun.

II

Summer cicadas sing on thick green
    stalks.
Dragonflies hover—like spirits—
    over
sunflower. Imagine the necessary
    joy
of perfect patterns, like circular
    sun-

flower seeds. Bees dance with pollen
   in
the space between seed and sun.

Is breath a pattern, like
   wind,
of movement?

III

Monsoon speaks with cottonwood
   leaf,
signs of the source. One leaf
   leads
the dance. Is it a mistake to
   revel
in the joy of each?

IV

I mistook grandeur for something
   more sublime
than dry arroyos and
   tiny seeds
but now I see the textile
   unfold
within me, within this
   desert.

Secrets of the seed
   link
my body to this world, these
   forms
of love, overjoyed, caught in the
   act
of symmetry.

V

If small thinking keeps us
    small,
what is small? Certainly not
    woolly bears
or nest of mourning doves. Not this
    morning
or any piece of celestial
    time.

We must announce our
    selves
to the sun. But, as soon as I start
    speaking in musts
I have stopped
    listening.

Japanese Garden

C. T. Holte

The myriad blossoms on the wisteria,
mammoth blooms on the tulip trees
and the tree whose name we do not know,
the rose garden—its first full glory
triggered by recent warm rains—
all contribute to the botanic rainbow.

The koi in the waterfall pond,
not yet fully roused from winter,
nose sluggishly in the mud near shore,
showing no favorites
as they pose seeking edible homage
from us or other pilgrims,
while wood ducks stare at us
from a nearby rock, safely out of reach.

The water spraying over the falls
says, Linger awhile.
*The afternoon breeze is soft
with the scent of roses.*

Water, sun, rocks, greenery all dazzle;
but the water is right: all other attractions,
however worthy of our attention,
are sidelined by the day's main event:
Lingering, under the sun.

Cottonwood

E. Griego-Montoya

The old grey cottonwood I met
on this morning's walk in the Bosque
didn't ask me
"why was I planted here?"

He did not complain
that his younger sister the elm
was growing so much closer to the Rio Grande.

He didn't worry
that he was not as tall or as straight
as his brother
who swayed in the wind
just a few yards away.

Every morning his towering figure
drinks deeply of the warm Burque sunlight
and in return, offers fresh cool oxygen
breathing life into the tiny sparrow
and the speckled butterfly.
So too for the coyotes and the roadrunners
who wander the trail near his mighty feet.

His twisted dark limbs
stretch eagerly toward the heavens,
seeking precious light from any direction
until they embrace the cobalt New Mexico sky.

The elder cottonwood knows
that each new season brings change.
He knows he will lose his shimmering leaves.
And that he will grow fresh ones.
A new branch here or a thick knot there.

Reminders of trials he's weathered.
His sturdy roots burrowing ever deeper every year
toward the moisture in the hard clay below.

He does not despair that one day
perhaps soon
he will be brought down
by a strong winter's storm,
or a spring's lightning strike
or a poor man's saw.

He might become a bench
where sweethearts sit together.
Or a stump
where a young boy will make his stand.
Or fuel for a fire
that will warm a family on a cold night.
Or nourishment
for the teeming life on the forest floor.

In the meadow nearby
a young green sapling
stretches her tiny arms
toward the warm summer sun.
She eagerly greets the new daylight.
It calls her closer.
Upward.
An inch at a time.
She too knows
she is planted
where she was meant to be.

Limpia (Burque Daze)

Bill Nevins

Cleansing memories of peeling chiles, stringing ristras,
Celebrating the iguana and Santana
I wend this road many years on
Whistling gabacho gypsy over the hill
Knowing that there may be no fond Spanish goodbye song
As Stephen Dedalus remarked in "Ulysses"
"We walk through ourselves . . .
But always meeting ourselves."
And I remember those tears,
Those laughs—Ay, dios mios!
Those South Valley sunsets
The waking to chicken crows and the question,
"Scrambled or juicy?"
The ghetto birds buzzing
Bullets tapping the tin roof
Of a New Years Eve or Independence Day,
The black widows lurking, pitbulls lunging,
Tequila shots, weddings, funerals,
Mad dog stares, black berets, smokey mota,
Flaunted bling, hidden guns and enchiladas
Slinging hay bales, breathing soft through warrior sweats,
And failing to learn how to make adobe bricks
The funerals and the healing ceremonies.
The curandera's poetry, mad as midnight.
The limpias and candles lit for the newly dead.
The prayers that were said as all prayers must be said
Gracias a dios y la Buena cosenada
panza llena corazon contenta
Can't complain.

Ode to Tony Mares

Mary Oishi

what is it i hear?
The Rio Grande weeping for her favorite son

yes, the Sandias whisper softly
he could have left us,
gone to sea level,
lived longer

march wind joins the mourning:
his roots so deep in this place
try as i may for seventy-six years to uproot him
it only made him stronger, deeper

disease at its deadliest could not dislodge

the mountains sigh, the river sniffs, the wind goes on

he left his footprints everywhere in poems
from Ghost Ranch to the Central Avenue Bridge
down dirt roads, in out-of-the-way hotels
to a hospital room too late to see her alive

i know, I followed him around, always over his shoulder

the river's tears now flowing hard

there, there don't cry, the wind consoles
as long as i blow across the desert high
as long as you, Sandias, stand sentinel in the east
as long as you, Rio Grande, flow through the bosque
Tony will still be here with us
in the pick-ups rolling down route 66
in the neighborhood bars, the coffee shops

the haunting calls of Sandhill Cranes
in the fuschias and lilacs of the setting sun

look up, listen, catch the scent of roasting green
Tony will always be here
the forever poet laureate of
the place between the mountains and the Rio Grande

Mujer de Mestizaje

Manuel González

Blue cloud
Yellow cloud
Rains down on the
thirsty sand

Madre Tierra stands
Exposed in her
beautiful vulnerability

Venus is the morning
star
Creation myth
Bearing our bloodlines
Sangre soaked soil
Choya and Chamisa
Fire
Famine and
Floods
She is in our blood
Her womb the ceremonial
bowl
Mujer de mestizaje
Carrying our pain and
creating cultura
Spider-Woman weaving
The entirety of all our
stories together
Tonantzin standing
beneath the sun
The weight of the world
on her brow
Holding our history in
her fingertips

The entirety of our
pigments on her skin

Our struggle is a holy
relic
Like turquoise placed
at her feet
Our bloodlines are her
story
Her medicine to heal
history

Coyolxauhqui moon
returns every month
To remind us of the
blood spilled
The cycles return
The wheel keeps spinning
The river keeps flowing
Night and day
Butterfly and moth
Mestizaje mixing sangre
Making us all familia

She is isis
She is gaia
Oshun
Oya
Yemaya

All our relations
come to celebrate
The road
The journey
The distance
Bloodlines
Beans
Black bears and

Hummingbirds
Flowers bloom
And
Coyote howls

Ancestral whispers
carried on the wind
Carried in our blood
Carried in her womb

Bosque

Sheryl Guterl

Quiet walkers, lost in thought,
create a symphony of footsteps,
pianissimo on soft sand.

Under fish-scale clouds,
sandhill cranes soar smoothly
over sage and sycamore,

their soft glissando drowned
out by staccato honking of Canadian geese,
in rhythm like a toddler with a new drum set.

Mallards float on glistening water.
River lips murmur praise to muddy bank
and majestic pampas grass.

Jackhammer downy taps aged cottonwood.
Dried leaves whisper their eulogies,
spirit songs through sun-kissed air.

Country Story

Jeremy Garcia

Upon hands that smallest lit window-board
Brings with it a forward march the spring wide
Motions to crisp, cold Morning-Glories
Sitting on the weekend mantel's flatness,
Still beams that balance the chill's rush
Of blushing atop a very sunken bloom.

So thoroughly flush with touch, and spread
Long as high, the lasting effect of late-quality
Roasts, fireplaces, painted wooden flute,
Rising halfway through the deep lights end,
Smoked-together, bent pieces of fields
and an empty ebony bathtub.

In a sling, a wavy bee leans on burnt petal fillings
Winning honey spoiled beneath the soaking soil.
The stinging troll was fast seen crossing colonies,
pastels, creamy trades, canvassed places treasuring
Warmth on top of lacy brushings, darkening at once.

Or, as in a second marriage, the old frame of a new picture
Above unmodern cusps of wanted seed spilled
Across windmills laid down, flowering together.

All aside summer's willing pushes this heavy
Reproduction of rights spreading into high homes,
Sky bringing a mild form of double ringing
To ears transitioning to larger eyeglasses,
Yelling about nature's buzz. The dry lift of cultured
Winds that sound young to any outside-looking fences
Nearly settled, reaches of the still womb.

Soon, before some weather's missing flares,
A normal flying crack: here rest babies jabbed, darted, and jeered,
Flown onto monsoons fighting at near odds in the city centering
While some fallen pollen tattoos highlight on the silver backs of apes.
So, too, goes the very tiny spreading of oldest wings beating evenly apart.

See common aims in level sights, here, so that scenery
Nurtures the strongest tips targeting the warm plateau's hole.
A rounding exchange for the spiral ascent of communications
In a gully so cut it speaks to bringing women in suits towards
A seemingly endless desk. Which would house the vase and stems
For every miniature cherry stone underneath it. As weights,
Fashionable brick cups carved from speaking fingers
Are left to wildly idle, a sea through blue shoring. Likewise,
Harvests of some scents of bottled rosy ships offer up
The deep-ended and stinging salute.

Remember, drag racers and closet queens, the little buggy
That poked through standards in reaching matchless honeycombs.
And by stepping from the bore hearts of redressed admirals,
It angered things by reading, "After the pictures of the general race develop."
Also, "A gender well of science" that broke in horse's drive,
Alternating colors of nuclear pants, and we matter to the cracklings
From an overreacting tinder box of global trends. We, in line,
Are just about the strange giant green thumbs of strangers.
Another flaming country story.

Galaxy Albuquerque

Mary Oishi

Albuquerque gradually flicks on scattered stars
throughout neighborhoods: street lights, porch lights
while the rose halo of the powerful star
still graces the horizon

behind the lesser stars below:
queens of their kitchens,
abuelitas with their hands in corn flour

mothers worry about their daughters
fathers feel proud of their children,
even those not theirs by blood

kids wish they were somewhere else
in a major galaxy like New York, Paris, L.A.
others bask in the glow of their forever home

an old woman's glad for her new puppy
who circles her like the moon
she calls her Luna

another woman gets the news she will be
a grandmother for the first time, anticipates
the brightest star she'll ever see

approaching stars, receding stars
passed out far from street lights,
flickering cold

stars about to blink out
in sacred rooms with hushed tones
glistening eyes

each star holds storied mysteries,
celebrations behind dancing lights:
we can't begin to know them all

tourists in the windowed restaurant
at the top of Sandia crest,
me in my stucco spaceship
docked in perfect position,
look out and take it in—
if the darkness holds pain
we can't see it—the
Galaxy of Albuquerque
sparkles across the night floor
its collection of lights
our own Andromeda:
peaceful,
magnificent, a
comfortable fiction of stars

On the Banks of the Rio Grande

Elsa Menendez

My hands as bowl or cup
for water.
Sifter for sand.
Molders of red summer mud.
My fingers as
paintbrushes.
On cheeks.
Into earth.
As direction givers.
Smoothers and soothers.
The harm they could cause.
Pokers. Pinchers.
Scratchers. Slappers. Scolders.
The peace they could find.
Thumb in mouth.
Hair twirlers. Doll
dressers. Tear wipers.
Touch my mama's cheek.
Tickle my brother's feet. Hold remnants of sticky sweets for me to lick after.
Hold.
Hold.
Reach.
Raise. Lift. Let go.
Squeeze. Wave. Signal.
Shush.
And when I lay on fallen
tree, on my back
With my head dangling off
one side and looking up
I could raise my hands
and trace the open spaces of the bosque ceiling.
Sky kingdom.
My fingers could

dance out dreams.
Untethered from
right-side-up my hands were portals to imaginary kingdoms.
View finders. Framers of
infinite possibilities.
Places where my magic
could heal
sadness or pain.
Wipe away rejection
or loneliness.
Rest
feeling loved and secure.
Hand on heart. Hand on
belly. Hands on hips.
Shake. Pray. Snap.
Extend. Caress. Cup.
Cover.
Tug. Revel. Reveal.
Linger.
Let go.
Hold.
Hold.
Hold.

Part Seven

Santa Tierra, Santo Sol

Watching Crow, Looking South Towards the Manzano Mountains

Joy Harjo

crow floats in winter sun
a black sliver
in a white ocean of sky
crow is the horizon
drifting south of Albuquerque
the horizon dances
along the blue edge
of the Manzanos
wind is an arch
a curve
on the black wing of crow
a warm south wind
if it stays for awhile
will keep a crow dancing for thirty years
on the ridge
of a blue mountain breeze

La Luz de Albuquerque

Linda Yiannakis

At dawn
the light awakens the Sandías,
flowing through the rocky crags,
spilling down upon the city
sheltered by those peaks,
and on the living ribbon
winding through the land.
Sol y río y bosque.
Three, but one together, too.

We walk the open trails,
the crunch of soil underfoot,
dry and pleasing to the ear.
Soil where once rolled the ancient seas,
where thunder lizards clashed and roared,
where angry mountains spewed out flames
consuming all before them.

Where ancient cultures came to life
and flowered in the desert;
the wail of prayer, the drone of chants,
the heartbeat pounding pulse of drums
all filled the desert air with song.
Three sounds, but one together, too.

Where strife and grief and conflict raged
in fierce and thunderous war,
with battle cries and flashing swords
did worlds collide in furious fray.

Yet centuries of time subdued
the seething battles on this land,

and as a city rose and grew
three cultures reached to touch and learn,
to share the light uniquely ours.
Three paths, but one together, too.

Fourteen Ways of Seeing Red Dragons Fly

Lenora Rain-Lee Good

Much new awaited me
when I moved to Duke City—
fry bread, no oxygen in the
thin air, dancing flame dragons
over the condo pond.

Not the blue and green
I knew, the ruby red
dragonflies stopped me cold
with their beauty and artistic dance.

Darting, flitting through
the sun, do they think
they are the Red Baron
reincarnated? Their aerial
dogfights ghostly quiet.

Dragonfly lust fulfilled,
they mate close to the water,
streams of fertilized eggs
coagulating in the pond.

Fall comes. Our pond
drained for winter.
What happens to all those eggs?
The little girl in me cries.

Next year more red flames
magically appear.
Happiness darts on
ruby red wings.

Spring comes. Sun
filters through trees,

dust motes dance with
red sparks of joy.

Would Baryshnikov have
studied the movements,
worn red sequined tights,
tried to dance with
their grace and agility?

Grandpa would have
made his own,
purchased wire and
feathers, beads and hook,
practiced his cast in the river.

No fish in our little pond,
only ducks to swim, mate,
make a mess. No bother
for our ruby fire dragons.

I never saw the flames
during the hail and
heavy rains of monsoons.
I never ventured out to look.

Small dragons, ruby brilliance
against green trees, reflected
in black water took my imagination
on dizzying rides.

When I'm not there
do the dragonflies miss me
sitting on the bench,
enjoying their ballet?

Am I now
woven into the cloth
of dragonfly mythology?

Burque

Adelio Lechuga-Kanapilly

Burque, home to us
Welcome to all

Hot sun burning into our skin
The river that cuts through our middle
That familiar sandy feel of stucco walls
Art that covers every corner of every building
This is Albuquerque
A hidden gem,
Nestled in the enchanting state

Burque, a safe place
For those from far away

Tough times
Meet tougher people
Carved in stone
By the ancestors they honor
Just a look in their eyes
Seems to say
"We are staying"

History woven in the strangest of places
The same streets
And the same people
Like a time loop that never ends
But this time, it's something you aren't sick of

Burque, a mix of culture and emotions
Our community
The one we've had since forever,
The one we make our own

A place for new beginnings
A place to preserve the historic
We are not a place to end

High Desert Blue (Bold and Fleeting)

PW Covington

As bold and fleeting
    as vapor-trails over Sandia Crest
You dance in my dreams
Dreams of things unmanifest
On diaphanous and shimmering wings

Holy homes and fall-out shelters beckon
Floods of quicksilver, rapid, river
Etch your eyes, your heels
    your lips and cigarettes
Into my mind

When we strolled beside the Bosque
New moon sky above cottonwoods
The only roof we knew, seeing through
Smoky cloud vapor masks

Mist, fog, steam
Hundreds of words for the
    next best thing

Prisms of promise swirl from
Our delta-wing, air base, aftermath
And, after that

Back to high desert blue
Bold and fleeting

Internal Argument with a Fellow Outsider

Alaina Davis

I never thought we would live in a place
where rainbow balloons
are an elemental part of the skyline.
Yet, here we are.

When I drive into work,
early, before the sun screams
over the crest of the mountain,
the city lights hold a mirror to the stars
that still dot the darkest parts of the sky.
Flickering yellow, beautiful.
Yet, they seem to know that daybreak
is about to steal their glory.

Then, the sunrise.
Spectacular magenta and orange
that cannot be captured
or adequately explained.
Attempting it often proves,
at best, animated,
at worst, disingenuous.

Lunch, and the cyan sky
is broken by clouds
that could not have been imagined
more perfectly
by an elementary school artist,
soft-white and non-threatening.

The mountains turn to watermelon
in the afternoon.
But everyone knows that.

When we moved here,
another transplant complained
that everything was too brown.

And, of course, there is brown.
We are guests in this desert.

But, there are also subtle shades
of sage and army green
that blend with the sepia
to provide more than adequate camouflage
for the agouti coyote that stalk the arroyo
on the other side of my fence.
Coral flowers line the streets of my neighborhood
shooting tall out of spikey green bushes,
and lavender grows in every other front yard.

When the moon returns to full each month,
it is somehow both creamy and bright,
like a bowl of buttermilk against the indigo of the night sky.

I never thought we would live in a place
where rainbow balloons
are an elemental part of the skyline.

Conversation

Gregory L. (Goyo) Candela

Petal-bursts of
purple Aster
orange-cupped
globe mallow—
among the profuse
fall bloom—border
the Bosque and
Aldo Leopold
Trails.
I greet them.

Arctic cold
descends on
Albuquerque.

The green cottonwood
canopy fades: first
choric yellow-leaf
clumps high in
each young crown; then
the duller leaves of older trees
spotted brown and
black, shiver
and die closer
to the ground.

Finally, throughout, the
clowns, motley leaves patched
yellow, green and gray.

Then the first
hard freeze
a mailed fist
slams down:

Cottonwood
leaves
shudder
turn brittle
an ancient
bronze armor
against
blue
steel.

Walt Simmons
frozen since
his fatal 2012
heart attack.
Hops on his ghost
bike and heads
South—

We chat
and—like the
flowers and
the trees—
he does not
talk back.

Wearing His Father's Dog Tags

Tina Carlson

The boy keeps sailing over the flooded fields
frothing with ditch: steam rising, hot ground under
the wet. Cottonwoods the width of a hut twist
into themselves, a century of bark.

He slips fingers into islands of slime, bays
where cool bugs hunker. He is small boy boat,
destination third grade, his arms beginning
to muscle. He hopes to see a Great White Shark

someday. He unclasps crawdads from the muck.
Smell of dead greens against the stile. The field
now pond with grain tips swimming. Air frills with
buzz and bite. Here in drought, water abounds.

Birthed from the first waters, his head was
soaped with sludge from the womb. The room:
full of ghosts. This boy gleams with tree sap,
sand glass, places sea sedge and carp

on the deck. He is hoisting the sail, departing
his shore. His father has long stopped waving.
His mother: steady as tree: beacon and branch.
The boy keeps sailing, a horizon they can't see.

Duke's Iron Sprawl

Timothy Reece Nelson

River run river run, slow and green.
Abounding verdant sea, arroyos around and around.

All around them here, the river flows
Among Dukes' iron sprawl, at their feet.

In the mountain's shadow, green serpent carves
spread lazily about itself, furious in flood.

Hidden in the green, horses and homes.
Down dusty roads the people live near.

The city always changes more and more
but the river, watched from olden churches

in its flow, seems to remain
forever and ever in time *gone* forever.

All around us, the river shall flow
until all is dust, at our feet.

Santa Tierra, Santo Sol

Irene Blea

Esta santa tierra warmed by santo sol
my sacred earth and sun
entities that heal and make things grow

More often now
it does not matter what I do not know
what counts is morning coffee on the patio
that clean air remains clean
green peas twine along a string
strawberries ripen red
a baby blue-tailed lizard feels safe enough
to exit from behind the shed

Blessed earth and sun
almas de mi vida
feed my soul

Good critters reside here
lady bugs and a desert tortoise
a few snails in this high arid desert
listen to my last night's dream
my water-colored goals
bumble bees buzz
here and there
they don't judge my uncombed hair

I smile at pink geraniums
check for insects on the squash
tomatoes and green beans hug trellises of corn stalk

On the patio cooling my swollen feet
a cordial current stirs
harmonic chimes recall

many summer days
it finally rained
I danced barefoot with two brown boys
I thank the hollyhocks
learned to nurture and let go

Gracias santa tierra
santo sol
for assisting me in growing old.

Day's End in February

Mary Dudley

The mountains lie like a watermelon
halved lengthwise,
their rose flesh glowing
in the setting sun.

West, across the valley,
the sky turns fuchsia first,
and then it's orange
and, finally, just a blush,

before I call the dogs
and close the gate
and go inside
to dinner.

One

Mark Goodman

Tell me it doesn't matter
The triple rainbows over the Manzanos

The red mountains
Leading down   from Española
Turn your back
On the Pink Sandias
The arroyo of the Rio Puerco
Tell the yellowed eyes
Peering from the sage

You won't be back
Because
You can never never
Leave

La Luz Trail

Madeline Aron

with songbirds
baroque concertos
crickets improvise
At the mountain base

of evolving sound
into centuries
We embark

my heart stretches hers
my feet snuggle into Redwings
awaken us:
Dawn's expectations

and solitary motifs
of occasional trills
is the sparse staccato
what's left on stage

under thickening green parasols
as boulder walls cool
muted crickets
laments replace

of solo virtuosity
into classic displays
music thins with air
As trees darken and lengthen

my heart flies
my legs tremble
to the peak
we climb again
falter
we climb

beckoning us to a higher ascent
with a single call to worship
cathedral caverns reverberate
promise the end
granite steeples

for us
an owl asks the question
into yearning
fatigue changes leisure

Home

Valerie Martínez

Once we claim it for ourselves, we've lost it forever.
A mystery we cannot own—where space begins.

Behind the coyote fence, adobe wall, blue window panes
is someone I do not know who calls this place home.

We tug at blue, at mountains, at easements.
We put our names on the ground, and sing.

It slips out of our hands.

•

You say it isn't ground but sky.
Unrolled to the skirt-hem of the horizon.

You say land is secondary to air.
As if we bed down, as if we float there.

Home is a parcel of sunlight
or moon-cooled air. Imagine:

everyone up off the ground, hovering.
Not this world, I'm afraid. Another one.

•

Not place, but people. I settle where you are,
where they have been, where you want to go.

It is the feeling of proximity, a nearness
in space. Locks of hair and fingernails

are intermediaries, interlocutors,
wooly hearth till the loved ones get home.

*

She says we carry it around inside, no matter.
Albuquerque, Chicago, Tucson, Swaziland.

He says: If only there were a way to make
the Sangres intestinal. She laughs.

*

Cellular, perhaps. Deep in the bone marrow,
muscles, DNA. Home is consanguineous,

tethering body to body, from here
to contention, every new creation story.

Blast of atoms, Eve's sudden appearance,
behind the mole who emerged from earth.

From *Father* up there to *Mother*
to *Matter*, down here. The spiral helix,

down from heaven, or climbing up,
root-like, from the center of the earth.

*

Tierra o muerte. Yes,
there are places worth
fighting for, if only
we could claim them,
definitively, forever until now.

As if nothing changed,
as if there was a single

defining document,
as if there is nothing
to be shared, and no one
was descended from us,
or wishes for something else.

To put my name
on this square foot
demands so much.

     •

When,
in my last hours,
when I forget
your face
and theirs
and everything
else, just lay me
down, here,
in her brown
and wrinkly
palms.

Albuquerque, New Mexico

Tani Arness

with gratitude to all the healers

We live in a city of 10,000 healers
we live in a city where the sky is a healer
the red mountain is a healer
and the moon rising over the mountain
and the stars moving round the moon
and the cottonwood trees and the sage
and creosote, coyotes, and crows.
We are surrounded by healers
and still we need more healers

We live in a city of strangers
kind strangers and confused strangers
we have memorized the difference
between fireworks and gunshots,
a city with stories on fire
and rain that needs to fall.
We walk out the door saying, Goodbye and Be safe.
Because this is a city of hurt people hurting people
and hurt people helping people.

We carry the earth in our bodies
like we carry gallons of water to leave in the desert
because we know
because the rocks know
and the sun knows, and the wind knows
that hurt people hurt people
and that is no excuse.

We live in a city of 10,000 healers
and still we need more healers.
We light candles and say,
Blessed are we who have been wrong,
who have been shattered and put together again,

blessed are the angry and the meek
and those running down the hillsides
in search of the river,
for we shall know God.

Part Eight

"Our Names Are Water, Our Names Are Mud"

A Collaborative Poem—Our Collective Voice—
with Lines from All the Poems in This Collection

One

Overhead *Bien Mur*, Big Mountain,
is alive with the evening's
watermelon promise.

Leave your offering
at the altar of the foothill.

Verdant, now, at sunup
each dust-mote drifter
is an atrium of bird-
wing vibrancy.

Do you feel your heart open?

Between the Sandias
and the volcanoes,
in the dry air of
our longing,
our names are water,
our names are mud.

Before the drizzle, who
brought the sky down?

Maybe we were the last place of strays,
the voices of hundreds in submission
sung in spirals.

We are not stones, you and I,
but dazzling tiny fish.

We try to track where we come from,
borders to match our veins.

We would like to be mirage and spectacle—
dry parched spaces, peeling
our lágrimas rojas, like a dozen red roses.

I too come from somewhere else.
Some of us have things inside
that could freeze the sun.

And yet sunlight begins to heal us.

Yes, the Sun, like a snot-nosed,
bratty kid.

Arc from sunrise to feldspar
pink at sundown.

Alive, atrium, mud, fish.
A dozen red sunsets.

Two

El tiempo, como Dios, se tarda pero no se le olvida.

The tense, present and fleeting, always has us
looking back to see how far we haven't gone.
It is a perfect union, like the cracks
and creases of human skin.

Beaming couples holding their newborns like collateral.

new life, new life, new life, new life, new life, new life

We never give up our roots, our gnarled cojones,
our underground brains.

Oh, Listener, you on the receiving end
of dust, snorting, thunder.

his thinker wouldn't make a teacup for a hummingbird

Nothing beneath the canopy reaches the sun,
which seems like an impossibility given the way
the sun touches down, with such vehemence,
by a native and self-nurturing love,

Quietly, I weep
for the Monarch butterfly.
I, an old man, cry.
Soy de ti y el otro.

Lighting up the trees a shimmering fire.

Three

In the year of our peril words have no meaning.

Pandemic hell, conspiracy hell,
mass shootings hell, history-erasing hell.

No one is here to save us.

Our lives are a cruise
down a broken highway.

We want paths to cut through the dry earth.
We want water.

So says the prophesy: our bloodlines, our story.

A young man on the threshold between
what is and what will be his life
walks el Bosque del Rio Grande
weary of the cycles. Almost blue.
Thinks: you can't top a mountain
as monstrous as a valley of land.

Like turquoise placed at his feet,
the tree bark, peeled back, reveals
the shape of a shaman, a healer, a doctor.

The desert doesn't get in the way of his view.

Imagine: your life in a glass box, healed
on the lands of our ancestors, one people
coming from all directions fill a vast diaspora.

My mountain taught me purpose and time.

Everything changes at the glow of dusk.
A body of water turns into a sea of lights,
we move from stardust to body.

En vez de coro, cigarra.
En vez de pila, río.

Color, and the noting it in our heads.

The billboard with our beautiful mountain:
Flatten the Curve.

Four

There were also two pink scars, both from her firebug phase,
and a black cloth riddled with holes. Way back then,
the life of the party left a legacy, a litter of cottonwoods.

The strange transformations that life undergoes in time.

But there's a simple beauty to the search; getting lost
in the scream of saws. Always the poor man building
the rich man's house with the best wood he can find.

There is wonderworking here from wherever
saints gather the holy man.

She is a poem, scrawled on a drum.

All those stars winking, as if in on a joke.
Tongues of magma, petroglyphs with messages.

The only place in America where Route 66 collides
with Route 66 as sunsets harvest the smoke, hear
the echoes, turn it breathtaking, turn it magic.

We are not a place to end.

The night parades its blue eloquence.
Melon mountains that rise from an empty sea.
A warm south wind.

Five

Waking to chicken crows and the question, "Scrambled or juicy?"
Like a whisper with a mission, secrets of the seed link my body to this world.
I live between a volcano and the edge of two tectonic plates.
Despite it all, there was still something alive beneath me.

Say: linger awhile, an inch at a time.

The elder cottonwood knows that each new season brings change.
River lips murmur praise to muddy bank and majestic pampas grass.
A new branch here or a thick knot there.

Look up. Listen. Catch the scent of roasting green.

We, in line, are just about the strange giant green
thumbs of strangers. Smoothers and soothers.
Albuquerque gradually flicks on scattered stars.

Shake. Pray. Snap. Extend. Caress. Cup.

Six

Where thunder lizards clashed and roared,
floods of quicksilver, rapid, river of sage
and army green blend with the sepia

Like a bowl of buttermilk
against the indigo of the night sky.

an ancient
bronze armor
against
blue
steel

Our struggle is a holy relic
when your body is a sieve
and re-beats your weary heart.

Air frills with buzz and bite, woven
into the cloth of dragonfly mythology?

Tell me it doesn't matter: crickets
improvise with a single call to worship,
an owl asks the question into yearning.

History woven into the strangest of places.

It does not matter what I do not know,
what counts is morning coffee on the patio
and, finally, just a blush.

River
run river
run, slow
and green

Home is
a parcel
of sunlight
or moon-cooled
air

Take home hope from wherever you can.

Tierra o muerte. Yes. Where
the sky is a healer because
the rocks know.

Acknowledgments

We would like to thank the City of Albuquerque and Mayor Tim Keller as well as the Department of Arts and Culture—staunch supporters of the literary arts—who have made this anthology possible.

Thanks to UNM Press for partnering on this and many other poetry books, especially Elise McHugh and Stephen Hull.

Thank you, Hakim Bellamy, for inspiring the title of this anthology with a line from your poem "ABQ Manifesto."

Thanks to our supportive circle of family and friends, always making time for our poetic endeavors, especially and always Paul and David.

Thank you to the many poets, past and present, who have been our inspiration, our mentors and students, our collaborators, guides, and companions.

About the Poets

Tani Arness grew up in rural Poulsbo, Washington, before moving to Albuquerque. The beauty of nature has always been a refuge for her and plays an important part in her creative work. Her prose and poetry can be found in numerous literary magazines including *North American Review, Red Rock Review, Green Mountains Review, Adobe Walls, Malpais,* and *Crab Orchard Review.* She thanks *The Paper* 1, no. 4 (2020), where "Albuquerque, New Mexico" first appeared in print.

Madeline Aron is a musician and healing artist residing in Albuquerque since 1974. She has a BGS from the University of Michigan and a BFA from the University of New Mexico. She is a member of Phi Beta Kappa. She produced a CD of New Mexican musicians called *In the Heart of the Wild Flame* that benefits environmental justice organizations. Most of her poetry resides in her songs.

Billy Babb is a native New Mexican, born in Albuquerque. He relocated to Albuquerque after years of living in Las Cruces and Denver. He is a husband, father, nurse, runner, music enthusiast, and lover of all things New Mexico. While earning his first degree at New Mexico State University, he dabbled in poetry. When word of this anthology came out, he thought this would be a perfect opportunity to share his love of running in the Albuquerque foothills.

Megan Baldrige studied Japanese literature at Yale, humanities at California State College, and education at the University of New Mexico. She homeschooled her own children for a few years, taught English to other people's children for twenty years, and taught GED classes recently. With the help of Jules' Poetry Playhouse, she has published five books of knitting poetry, a book of poems about our former president, and one about her late dog. Her poetry book *Knitting Matters* won a best crafts book award in 2019, and her *Unpresidented* was a finalist for political books in the New Mexico–Arizona Book Awards in 2018. She led the NMSPS Poets in the Classroom project in 2019 and works as a docent at the Albuquerque Museum. She likes to grow flowers, tutor children, knit sweaters, write lighthearted poetry, and walk in the bosque.

Hakim Bellamy is a multifaceted, multidisciplinary artist and arts leader who served as the Inaugural Poet Laureate of Albuquerque from 2012 to 2014. His poetry has been published on the Albuquerque Convention Center, on the outside of a library, in inner-city buses, and in numerous anthologies across the globe. His first book, *Swear*, won the Tillie Olsen Award for Creative Writing from the Working Class Studies Association. Bellamy has had his work featured in Rattle, AlterNet, Truthout, CounterPunch and on the nationally syndicated Tavis Smiley Radio Show. His most recent publication is *Commissions y Corridos: Poems*.

Irene Blea is a native New Mexican and a writer of textbooks, poetry, and novels. She retired as a tenured full professor in and the chairperson of Chicano and Chicana Studies at California State University–Los Angeles and returned to the land of her birth to write family stories, tend to her flower beds, and watch her teenage granddaughter mature. She is a celebrated author of sociology textbooks and a public speaker and is active with the New Mexico Humanities Council.

Gregory L. (Goyo) Candela, professor emeritus at the University of New Mexico, has published two volumes of poetry—*Surfing New Mexico* and *Shallow Rooted Heart*—and written six produced plays (including a radio play for KUNM, *El Mozo Regresa*). His recent publications include poems in the *Harwood Anthology*, the *Malpaís Review*, *Adobe Walls*, and *Sin Fronteras* as well as in *Circe's Lament*, an anthology of poems about women.

Tina Carlson is the author of three previous collections of poetry: *A Guide To Tongue Tie Surgery*; *Ground, Wind, This Body*; and *We Are Meant To Carry Water*, a collaboration with two other New Mexico poets. She has lived in Albuquerque for over thirty years and worked at Albuquerque Healthcare for the Homeless as a nurse practitioner.

Carlos Contreras is a poet, artist, father, educator, and student. He was a member of the Kellogg Foundation's Inaugural class of Community Leadership Network Fellows. He has worked in various nonprofits and also served as the director of marketing and innovation with the City of Albuquerque. Contreras is a nationally awarded performance poet and a published author. His poetry/painting is currently included in the exhibition *Common Ground* at the Albuquerque Museum.

Crystal Coriz is a high school student at the Native American Community Academy (NACA). She was born and raised in Albuquerque but comes from Gallup and Santo Domingo Pueblo. In carrying both her Navajo and Keres heritage, she hopes to use poetry to guide future generations to share their voices, passions, and understandings, because there is more than one purpose, and the first starts with you.

PW Covington writes in the Beat tradition of the North American highway. His short fiction collection *North Beach and Other Stories* was named an LGBTQ Fiction finalist by the International Book Awards in 2019. Covington lives two blocks off of Historic Route 66 in Albuquerque, New Mexico.

A native of Albuquerque's South Valley, **Jasmine Sena Cuffee** has been active in the arts community for almost twenty years as a performance and spoken-word artist. She has led writing workshops and performed throughout New Mexico and the Western United States for grades K–12 and beyond. Her work is included in the *Bigger Boat Anthology, Earthships: A New Mecca Poetry Anthology, ¿De Veras?*, and the *Malpais Review*.

Alaina Davis is a lawyer, mom, and wife as well as an occasional artist and a part-time baker with two adorable baking assistants, aged four and nine. Her family is originally from Kansas City, but she has called Albuquerque home since 2019. She loves looking for coyotes in the arroyo behind her house and watching balloons early in the morning.

Mary Dudley's work has been published in *Sin Fronteras* and *Adobe Walls Journals*, in the *poets speak* and *Fixed and Free* anthologies, and in other collections including *Value, Missing Persons, 22 Poems & a Prayer for El Paso*, and *Civilization in Crisis: An Anthology of Poetic Response*. She has published three chapbooks, most recently *Be Still*.

Every year since 2009, **EKCO** (Ekphrastic + Collaboration) has engaged groups of women poets to write and co-create original poetic performances, often in response to art. EKCO integrates literary poetry with performance in order to elevate and energize the role of poetry in contemporary life. EKCO was founded by Valerie Martínez in 2009. She was joined by Shelle VanEtten de Sánchez as co-coordinator in 2011. Visit www.artful-life.org to learn more.

Jamie Figueroa is the author of the novel *Brother, Sister, Mother, Explorer*. She is Boricua (Afro-Taíno) by way of Ohio and a longtime resident of northern New Mexico. Her writing has appeared in *American Short Fiction, Emergence Magazine, Elle, McSweeney's,* and *Agni,* among others. She received a Truman Capote Award and was a Bread Loaf Rona Jaffe Scholar. A VONA alum, she received her MFA in creative writing from the Institute of American Indian Arts.

Mark Fleisher has published three books of poetry (with prose and photographs included) and collaborated on a fourth. His work has appeared in numerous online and print publications in the United States, Canada, the United Kingdom, Kenya, Nigeria, South Africa, and India. He received a journalism degree from Ohio University. Fleisher's service in the United States Air Force included a year in Vietnam where he was awarded a Bronze Star.

Damien Flores is an award-winning poet, teacher, and radio host, born and raised in Old Town, Albuquerque. He is best known as a member of the three-time national champion Albuquerque Poetry Slam Team, a troupe of competitive spoken-word artists who represent the Duke City in poetry slam tournaments across the United States. He is an experienced teacher of twelve years and is the head producer and host of The Spoken Word Hour on 89.9 KUNM-FM.

Carolyn Fresquez has an MSc in dance movement psychotherapy and a BA in creative studies, literature. She has worked with kids and youth in dance studios, theaters, special schools, and incarceration facilities, teaching dance and choreography as well as leading movement and therapy sessions. She has also worked with adults in a variety of settings in both creative and therapeutic capacities.

Jeremy Garcia writes, "My name is Jeremy Garcia, but to family and friends, it's just J ("Jay"). This is the second time I've submitted anything I've written. Only as a hobby do I ever write or do poems. And I, like many others, have had some exposure to Albuquerque poetry and English students and teachers in general. Thank you for reading my thoughts, and a special thanks for the thoughts of other poets."

Originally from Albuquerque, New Mexico, **Olivia Gatwood** has received international recognition for her poetry, her writing workshops, and her work as a Title IX compliant educator in sexual assault prevention and recovery. Olivia's performances have been featured on HBO, Huffington Post, MTV, VH1, and BBC, among others. Her poems have appeared in the Poetry Foundation, the Sundance Film Festival, Lambda Literary, and the *Missouri Review* as well as elsewhere. She is the author of two poetry collections, *New American Best Friend* and *Life of the Party*, and the novel *Whoever You Are, Honey.*

Manuel González served as the Poet Laureate of Albuquerque from 2016 to 2018. A performance poet who began his career in the poetry slam, Manuel has represented Albuquerque four times as a member of the ABQ Slam Team at the National Poetry Slam. Manuel has appeared on the NMPBS show *Colores: My Word is My Power*, and he is one of the founding members of the poetry troupe *The Angry Brown Poets*. Manuel teaches workshops on self-expression through poetry in high schools and youth detention centers. He has also worked with art therapists to help incarcerated young men find an outlet to express themselves.

Lenora Rain-Lee Good lives by the Columbia River in Richland, Washington. She loved her time in Albuquerque but couldn't adjust to the altitude. Her latest collection of poems, prose, and memoir is *A Bride's Gate and Other Assorted Writings*. Her poems have appeared in *Cirque*, *Quill & Parchment*, *Poet's Brew*, and the *WA129* anthology collected by then–Washington poet laureate Tod Marshall. She is a member of New Mexico State Poetry Society, Albuquerque Chapter.

Mark Goodman is a fourth-generation New Mexican Originally from Belen, he currently lives in Albuquerque. He has lived in the state off and on since being born in Belen, when they had a hospital. He has used Belen, Albuquerque, and the railroad towns as his "triggering towns."

E. Griego-Montoya is a native Burqueño and a recovering politico who studies, teaches, and consults on public-policy issues. He currently lives with his wife, son, and two pandemic pups in the Barelas home where he was raised. When he's not working he enjoys playing his guitar, walking in the Bosque, and wading in the Rio Grande.

Sheryl Guterl writes from New Mexico and New Hampshire. Having retired to the Southwest after a career as an educator in New Jersey, she appreciates more sunshine, higher mountains, and less winter ice. Her cabin on a lake in wooded New England provides inspiration and refreshment with cooler summers. Sheryl's poetry can be found in the *Ravens' Perch*, the *Iris Literary Journal*, *Deep Wild*, the *Bethlehem Writers' Roundtable*, and several local anthologies.

Tanesia R. Hale-Jones is an educator, poet, and artist. Tanesia is passionate about creative collaboration, which includes her work and performances with EKCO poets and the poetry/textile collaboration she did with local artist Maude Andrade, "Romance and Necessary Fictions." She also served on the Organizing Committee for the Albuquerque Poet Laureate Program. She has performed her original poetry at Tricklock Performance Space, Harwood Art Center, Burque Noir, and Chatter. Her written work has been published in *callaloo*, *Sentence 5*, *14 Hills*, and *Mirage#4/Period(ical)* and has been featured in multiple exhibitions at Harwood Art Center. Tanesia lives and creates on Tiwa Territory (also called Albuquerque).

Joy Harjo is an internationally renowned performer and writer of the Muscogee (Creek) Nation. She served three terms as the twenty-third Poet Laureate of the United States from 2019 to 2022. The author of nine books of poetry (including the highly acclaimed *An American Sunrise*), several plays and children's books, and two memoirs (*Crazy Brave* and *Poet Warrior*), her many honors include the Ruth Lily Prize for Lifetime Achievement from the Poetry Foundation, the Academy of American Poets Wallace Stevens Award, two NEA fellowships, and a Guggenheim Fellowship. As a musician and performer, Harjo has produced seven award-winning music albums including her newest, *I Pray for My Enemies*.

C. T. Holte grew up in Minnesota without color TV; played along creeks and in cornfields; went to lots of school; and has had gigs as a teacher, an editor, and doing less wordy things. He recently migrated to New Mexico and got a cool electric chainsaw for Christmas. His poetry has been published in *Words*, *California Quarterly*, *Months to Years*, *Pensive*, the *Daily Drunk*, *Mediterranean Poetry*, and elsewhere, and has been hung from trees to celebrate the Rio Grande Bosque.

Anushah Jiwani is a Pakistani American poet based in Albuquerque. Anushah believes stories are avenues for healing. Through her work as a social-justice advocate, a life coach, and a facilitator, Anushah has been fulfilling her dream to create a liberating space for BIPOC individuals. Much of Anushah's writing centers on her Pakistani American identity and aims to create spaces for immigrant voices.

Feroza Jussawalla is a professor emerita from the University of New Mexico. She has lived and taught in Albuquerque since 2001 and has been active on the Victory Hills Neighborhood Association board. She is the author and co-editor of several books, primarily on postcolonial literatures, including her collection of poems, *Chiffon Saris*. Most recently she has co-edited *Memory, Voice, and Identity: Muslim Women's Writing from across the Middle East*.

Maiyah King is a poet and artist. She is a proud member of the Navajo Nation and also has Pueblo of Acoma ancestry. She has been a poet with *RezSpit*, an Indigenous Youth Poetry Collective that highlights the lived experiences of Native people. Maiyah is an alumni of the Soul of Nations Foundation, through which she has participated in the 2018 Native Collegiate Artist Residency and the Soul of Nations Group Exhibition at Santa Fe Indian Market.

Zachary Kluckman is a Scholastic Art and Writing Awards Gold Medal Poetry Teacher, an organizer with the 100 Thousand Poets for Change program, and a 2021 Thomas Lux scholar. Recently he was one of three American poets invited to the Kistrech International Poetry Festival. Kluckman is the founder of MindWell Poetry, which is dedicated to creating safe spaces and advocating for those who have been marginalized due to mental-health experiences, and he has authored two previous poetry collections.

Adelio Lechuga-Kanapilly is an artist and poet from Albuquerque, New Mexico. He is published in '22 Poems and a Prayer for El Paso and has worked on various projects throughout the city with other Albuquerque artists. He enjoys crocheting, reading, and hanging out with his cats in his free time.

Maria L. Leyba has lived in her family home in Barelas for seventy-two years. She has watched the changes in our magnificent city over the years, from dirt streets to indoor plumbing, the wars, and into the present. She writes to keep the memories of our life alive.

Jessica Helen Lopez was the City of Albuquerque's second Poet Laureate. Her books of poetry are *The Blood Poems, Always Messing with Them Boys, Cunt. Bomb.*, and *The Language of Bleeding: Poems for the International Poetry Festival, Nicaragua*. She is the host of the PBS show *¡COLORES!*—a weekly art series with stories devoted to the creative spirit. Lopez is also an award-winning slam poet and holds the title of 2012 and 2014 Women of the World City of ABQ Champion. She is a member of the Macondo Foundation and the founder of *La Palabra—The Word Is a Woman*, a collective created for and by women and gender-identified women.

Anna C. Martínez is a local civil-rights attorney, a performance poet, and a mother and grandmother raised in Española, New Mexico, and living in Albuquerque. Her work was first published in the 2014 anthology *La Palabra: The Word Is a Woman*, and also in *Lowriting: Shots, Rides and Stories from the Chicano Soul*. Her first book of poetry, *Pura Puta: A Poetic Memoir*, was released in 2022. Anna has held titles as ABQ Haiku Champ, Chicano/a Slam Champ, and 2019 City Slam Champ of Mindwell Slam. She is currently serving as the sixth Albuquerque Poet Laureate from 2022 to 2024.

Valerie Martínez is a poet, educator, arts administrator, and collaborative artist. Her six books of poetry include *Absence, Luminescent*; *World to World*; and *Each and Her*. Her most recent work, *Count*, is a book-length poem that addresses the devastating effects of climate change. Martínez was the Poet Laureate for Santa Fe from 2008 to 2010. She is the founding director of Artful Life (www.artful-life.org) and the founder of the EKCO poetry collaborative, which has been creating spoken-word performances since 2009. Albuquerque has been her home since 2005. The poem "Home" was previously published, in slightly different form, in *And They Called It Horizon: Santa Fe Poems*.

Mary McCray's books, *Why Photographers Commit Suicide* and *Cowboy Meditation Primer*, were finalists in the 2013 and 2019 Indie Excellence Awards. *Cowboy Meditation Primer* was a finalist in the New Mexico/Arizona Book Awards and the Nautilus Book Awards. She has produced Cher zines and blogs as Cher Scholar and runs the poetry blog Big Bang Poetry (which includes the year-long, meditative writing project "52 Haiku"). The poem "Imagine Mars" was previously published in *Why Photographers Commit Suicide*.

Don McIver, winner of the Basic Human Needs poetry award, is a six-time member of the ABQ slam team, where he participates as a poet and a coach; a host/producer of KUNM's *Afternoon Freeform*; the author of *The Noisy Pen* and *The Blank Page*; and an editor of *A Bigger Boat: The Unlikely Success of the Albuquerque Poetry Slam Scene*. He's a teacher by trade at Central New Mexico Community College, where he also manages the tutoring center.

Elsa Menendez is a performer, writer, director, circus artist, and producer. As a facilitator, educator, and artist her passion is to connect through story and play and to co-create in intercultural environments with diverse groups of collaborators. Elsa currently serves as the deputy director for the City of Albuquerque's Department of Arts & Culture.

Susan Mitchell embraces folklore, ghosts, and monsters. She tunes into that wavelength to write poetry, horror, and thrillers. She really likes books, music, road trips, thrift stores, and horror movies. Susan has a degree in English from Northern Arizona University, and her work has appeared in some brave literary magazines.

Elaine Carson Montague co-authored *Victory from the Shadows: Growing Up in a New Mexico School for the Blind and Beyond*, which was awarded first place for biography in 2020 by the National Federation of Press Women. It documents how Gary lived successfully with lifelong low vision and struggled with education and employment prior to ADA, and it presents domestic life on the eastern plains of New Mexico in the mid-twentieth century. She writes from the heart and loves God, mountains, sunsets, and New Mexico chile.

Rene Mullen is the managing editor for a public-relations firm in Albuquerque, a performance and traditional poet, the author of the full-length poetry collection *This Still Breathing Canvas*, and the host of the Pen and Poet podcast. His poetry has been featured in *Poetry Quarterly*, *50 Haikus*, and the *Santa Fe Literary Review*.

R. Naso currently lives in Albuquerque, New Mexico.

Timothy Reece Nelson is a writer and poet inspired by diversity and the bonds people make through their devices and lives. His most recent poems and writing pieces are published on Patreon under the username BungieONI. After receiving a BA in chemical engineering from the University of New Mexico, he channeled his passion for writing into a hobby until the COVID-19 pandemic struck, and then he took the lockdowns as an opportunity to follow that passion.

Bill Nevins has studied under the guidance of poets Stephen Spender, Epifanio San Juan Jr., Terence Winch, Kell Robertson, and others. He has been an educator in secondary schools and colleges, including at Central New Mexico Community College and the University of New Mexico; a psychiatric social worker; a factory hand; a firewood cutter; a progressive political activist and war resistor; a gold-star parent and grandparent; a publishing journalist; a filmmaker and film subject; an editor; and a poet. He is the author of *Heartbreak Ridge*, *Mammal-Fish*, and *Selected Poems*.

Jenna L. Norton is a social worker, therapist, and mountaineer. She resides in Albuquerque, New Mexico.

Jules Nyquist is the founder of Jules' Poetry Playhouse in Placitas, New Mexico, a place for poetry and play. Jules' Poetry Playhouse was founded in Albuquerque in 2012. Her latest book is *Atomic Paradise*, an exploration of growing up in the Cold War and living in the Land of Enchantment surrounded by nuclear secrets. She served on the Albuquerque Poet Laureate Selection Committee from 2016 to 2017.

Mary Oishi served as the Poet Laureate of Albuquerque from 2020 to 2022. Oishi is the author of *Sidewalk Cruiseship: Poems* and *Spirit Birds They Told Me* and the co-author of *Rock Paper Scissors*, which was finalist for the New Mexico–Arizona Book Award. She is one of twelve US poets in translation in *12 Poetas: Antología De Nuevos Poetas Estadounidenses*, a project of the Mexican Ministry of Culture. Her poems have appeared in *Mas Tequila Review*, *Malpais Review*, *Harwood Anthology*, and numerous other print and digital publications. Oishi worked professionally and as an on-air personality in public radio for twenty-five years, hosting blues shows at four radio stations in New Mexico and Colorado.

Bill O'Neill grew up in rural Ohio and graduated from Cornell University. Elected to the New Mexico Legislature in 2008, he is now in his second term in the New Mexico State Senate. His poems have appeared in numerous literary reviews, both regional and national. Bill's career has been framed by his work with nonprofits, with a focus on incarcerated juveniles and adults. In 2005 Governor Bill Richardson appointed him executive director of the New Mexico Juvenile Parole Board. Named an Emerging Leader in 2016 by the University of Virginia's Darden School, he credits his early literary inspiration to mentors E. L. Doctorow and V. B. Price.

Michelle Otero is the author of *Vessels: A Memoir of Borders*; *Malinche's Daughter*, an essay collection based on her work as a Fulbright Fellow with women survivors of domestic violence and sexual assault in Oaxaca, Mexico; and *Bosque: Poems*, a collection written during her tenure as Albuquerque Poet Laureate from 2018 to 2020. She is a member of the Macondo Writers Workshop.

Peter Pachak-Robie is a multi-instrumental, multi-genre–loving, diverse experience–seeking devourer of the bizarre and mystifying. He is currently teaching young musicians in Albuquerque how to make weird sounds with computers.

V. B. Price received the 2021 New Mexico Literary Arts Gratitude Award for "contributions to the life of the poetry community in New Mexico and the Southwest." He has been publishing poetry since 1962. His column on politics, culture, and the environment has appeared virtually every week for the last fifty-two years, and it currently runs at mercmessenger.com. He taught for many years in the University of New Mexico Honors College and the School of Architecture and Planning. His twenty-five books include *Innocence Regained: Christmas Poems*, *Chaco Body*, and *Memoirs of the World in Ten Fragments*.

Sylvia Ramos Cruz's writing is inspired by art, women's lives, and everyday injustices. Her work reflects her life in Puerto Rico, New York, and New Mexico. Her award-winning photographs, prose poetry, and historical essays have appeared in local and national publications, including *Southwestern American Literature*, *PoetryBay*, *Chamisa Journal 2021*, and *Artemis 2021*. She is a retired breast surgeon, a world traveler, and a women's rights activist still working to get the Equal Rights Amendment into the Constitution.

Margaret Randall is a poet, feminist, photographer, oral historian, and social activist. Born in New York City in 1936, she has lived for extended periods in Albuquerque, New York, Seville, Mexico City, Havana, and Managua. She moved to Mexico City in the 1960s, where she co-founded and co-edited the bilingual literary journal *El Corno Emplumado / The Plumed Horn*. From 1984 through 1994 she taught at a number of US universities. She is the author of more than one hundred books of poetry, prose, oral testimony, and memoir. Her most recent works include *Time's Language: Selected Poems 1959–2018*, *I Never Left Home: Poet, Feminist, Revolutionary*, and *My Life in 100 Objects*.

Cal Reardon is a lifelong Albuquerque resident, with a small hiatus by way of Prescott College. He can often be found with a hot-air balloon crew or walking through the bosque with his Labrador. His work has previously appeared in *Oakland Arts Review*, *Albion Review*, and *Alligator Juniper*.

Levi Romero is from the Embudo Valley of New Mexico, and he earned a BA and an MA in architecture at the University of New Mexico. A bilingual poet whose language is immersed in the regional manito dialect of northern New Mexico, Romero is the co-author of *Sagrado: A Photopoetics Across the Chicano Homeland* and the author of *A Poetry of Remembrance: New and Rejected Works*, *In the Gathering of Silence*, and other publications. Romero was named the centennial poet for New Mexico for 2012, an honorary post, and he also served as the inaugural New Mexico Poet Laureate from 2020 to 2022. The poem "Azucarero" was inspired by Afton Love's *Perfect Union* and Neal Ambrose-Smith's *The (Tense) Present*, concurrent exhibits at 516 Arts in the Spring of 2021 in Albuquerque.

Monica Sánchez has followed her bliss throughout a life in the theatre and the theater of life. For over thirty years she has honed the craft of professional actor (SAG/AFTRA, AEA); written and devised work collaboratively and independently for the stage; directed a handful of productions small and large; and enjoyed a myriad of assignments as a teaching artist and community-engagement facilitator with diverse and intergenerational communities. She holds an MFA in dramatic writing from the University of New Mexico.

Born in Colorado, **Alissa Simon** attended the University of New Mexico. She also has degrees from Arizona State University and Harrison Middleton University, where she is currently a tutor. She also works with the Viridis Graduate Institute. Alissa hikes as often as possible in the beautiful New Mexican landscapes. She also enjoys reading and writing. She is passionate about literature and discusses all types of media whenever possible. She blogs at hmu.edu.

Jeff Sims grew up in Los Lunas, New Mexico, as the middle child of divorced parents. He graduated from the University of New Mexico and began a life living and working outdoors, making his way from the desert waters of the Southwest to the far verdigris streams of Alaska. Eventually, after many years spent in the north, he returned home to the city he has grown to love.

Ryan M. Stark is a graduate of the University of New Mexico's creative writing program, where he studied under Lee Bartlett, Patricia Clark Smith, and Marcia Southwick. In addition to writing poetry, Stark has worked extensively in the nonprofit field, served as a search-and-rescue aircrew member, and writes music. He resides with his wife and three children in Albuquerque's South Valley.

Originally from Chicago, **Janet St. John** has lived in Albuquerque for nearly twenty years. She has an MFA in poetry from Vermont College, and her poems and short fiction have been published in numerous literary journals, including the *Nebraska Review*, *Passages North*, the *Ekphrastic Review*, *bosque*, *ABQinPrint*, *Puerto del Sol*, *StepAway*, and *After Hours*. Two of her prose poems were exhibited as part of the *Art & Words* Collaborative Show in Dallas, Texas.

Shelle VanEtten de Sánchez is an organizer, educator, creative facilitator, and optimist living happily with her family in Barelas. She has more than thirty years of professional experience and leadership in arts, culture, education, and public service in a variety of spaces, including classrooms, higher education, cultural institutions, entrepreneurship, nonprofits, and government. She also makes time to write, make, and collaborate on a variety of creative projects as often as possible (but not as often as she would like!).

A 2021 inductee into the Texas Institute of Letters, **Scott Wiggerman** is the author of three books of poetry, *Leaf and Beak: Sonnets*; *Presence*; and *Vegetables and Other Relationships*. He is also the editor of *Wingbeats I & II: Exercises & Practice in Poetry* and *22 Poems and a Prayer for El Paso*, winner of a New Mexico–Arizona Book Award in 2020. Wiggerman has most recently published poems in *El Palacio*, *Naugatuck River Review*, and *Modern Haiku*.

Linda Yiannakis is a retired speech-language pathologist, who spent over thirty years helping people with a wide variety of communication disorders. She has had a special interest in language and literacy and has always enjoyed writing. Linda holds sixth-degree black belts in both Traditional Kodokan Judo and Japanese Jujutsu, and she has published several technical articles as well as book chapters related to these arts. In addition, she has published two middle-grade novels, *Erasable* and *Digby of The Dinosaurs*.

ONE
ALBUQUE
RQUE   arts & culture

The Albuquerque Poet Laureate Series

Co-published with the City of Albuquerque's Department of Cultural Services, the Albuquerque Poet Laureate Series features new and selected work by the city's Poet Laureate at the conclusion of their two-year term. Newly appointed poets will join Hakim Bellamy, Jessica Helen Lopez, Manuel González, Michelle Otero, and Mary Oishi as significant voices in the community who have been recognized with the honor of serving as the Poet Laureate and sharing their craft in the volumes published in the series.

Also available in the Albuquerque Poet Laureate Series:

Sidewalk Cruiseship: Poems by Mary Oishi
Commissions y Corridos: Poems by Hakim Bellamy
The Blood Poems by Jessica Helen Lopez
Bosque: Poems by Michelle Otero
Duende de Burque: Alburquerque Poems and Musings by Manuel González